GENERATIONAL WEALTH BUILDER

GENERATIONAL WEALTH BUILDER

BUILDING SUCCESS WHILE ENJOYING LIFE

JOE AUSTIN II

For information about this title or to order other books and/or electronic media, contact the publisher:

Joe Austin II
24624 I-45 North, Ste 200 | Spring TX 77386
joeaustinii.com

ISBN:
978-1-7337813-0-5 (Hardcover)
978-1-7337813-1-2 (Softcover)
978-1-7337813-2-9 (eBook)

Printed in the United States of America

Joe Austin II is a retired United States Air Force Major and an entrepreneur who has started transportation and real estate companies. Currently, he is the Owner of Austin Luxury Realty Services, a company that assists buyers and sellers with their residential, commercial, land, and investment needs. Joe has a passion for increasing financial knowledge and encouraging others to pursue their dreams, and he leads Home Buying & Wealth Building Cohort for individuals who desire to purchase real estate and better their financial position. Joe is also passionate about fighting breast cancer since his mother, Sylvia Austin, lost her battle to the disease when he was only six years old.

Joe's father, Joe Sr, definitely taught Joe financial responsibility at an early age. By the time Joe was in junior high school, he was responsible for purchasing his school supplies, clothes, putting money in a savings account, and giving his offering to his church.

Joe enlisted in the Air Force during his senior year of high school as a delayed enlistee, and within two months of graduating, he was in basic training at Lackland AFB in San Antonio, Texas. He went on to have assignments at Keesler AFB in Biloxi, Mississippi, and Offutt AFB in Omaha, Nebraska. While at Offutt, Joe earned a bachelor's degree from the University of Nebraska at Omaha in aviation studies. He also earned a private pilot's license and has over one hundred hours of flight time. Initially, he longed to become an Air Force pilot; however, despite being accepted for the program, roadblocks appeared along the way and changed his destiny. He still yearns to fly, and he still loves to zip through the air in a private aircraft. After completing Officer Training School at Maxwell AFB in Montgomery, Alabama, Joe was assigned to Scott AFB in Illinois near St. Louis, Missouri. He was an Aircraft Maintenance Officer with the C-9A Nightingale unit. He often encouraged people to invest, go to school, and have good work habits in order to succeed in life. Joe's additional assignments include Robins AFB, Georgia, the Naval Postgraduate School where he earned a Master's of Business Administration Degree in Acquisition and Contract Management, Lackland AFB, Texas, and Greenville, Texas. Joe elected an early retirement at the age of thirty-six after serving in the Air Force for more than eighteen years.

Joe is an avid researcher of financial topics and has read many books and publications by various authors. He also authored financial publications as a financial contributor for *Epitome Magazine*. Some of those topics are subjects in this book. He hopes this book will open the doors to a topic many don't focus on. Joe is available to do workshops and seminars, and to provide help wherever needed. He is particularly interested in personal and non-profit finances. Joe is a firm believer that if individuals are financially independent, they will be able to live more comfortable lives and will be able to support their local community in a stronger manner.

DEDICATION

I dedicate this book to my loving family who has supported me along the way through all of my ideas, aspirations, and military career. No matter what I have in my heart to accomplish, you always encourage me.

I also thank my extended family and friends who provided some of the foundation during the early, trying part of my life. I realize some have passed away, and I am truly grateful for them and their families as well.

I am also appreciative to everyone who has come into my path during various personal and professional stages of my life. Your encouragement, mentoring, and kind words have meant so much to me. If it had not been for your actions, I would not have gained the wisdom that allowed me to achieve the level of success I'm blessed with.

Last but not least, I dedicate this book to my loving mother, Sylvia Austin. Even though you lost your battle to breast cancer when I was six years old, I hope that I have made you proud. I love you, Mom!

FOREWORD

Charles Goldsmith

Joe Austin II contacted me on various occasions for mentoring and guidance. I have a sincere appreciation for his desire to learn and to help others with the vast financial knowledge he has acquired over the years.

As a national sales director with Primerica Financial Services, I know first-hand the importance of this information. As a financial analyst, business owner, and real estate investor for over thirty years, I know the value of financial planning, managing assets, and growing your personal net worth.

My group of personal financial analysts spans fifteen offices in Texas, Louisiana, and Georgia, and we assist many individuals, families, and businesses with financial strategies for life insurance, annuities, mutual funds, long-term care, 401(k) plans, and several debt elimination strategies.

Generational Wealth Builder attempts to help people improve their financial wellbeing. The book encourages the reader to do better by providing simple strategies that can easily be implemented. The main point is to have a changed mind. Once you determine that you desire to do better, you'll have greater success not only with your finances but throughout your life!

Joe Austin II has vast experience both professionally and personally. His eighteen-plus years in the Air Force allowed him to see various places while accomplishing tasks many civilians will never have the opportunity to witness. During this time, he earned his associate's, bachelor's, and master's degrees. The interesting fact is that he only accumulated $8,000 in student loans, which was taken out in order for him to obtain his private pilot's license. Even early in his career, he remained focused on putting himself on the proper path to enjoy the benefits later in life. He previously provided financial guidance in his book, *Money Grows on Trees . . . If You Plant the Right Seeds. Generational Wealth Builder* is a follow-up book that provides additional guidance for the reader to gain more in-depth understanding of finances in a simple way.

Joe is an avid teacher of the financial gospel. As a real estate broker, he educates homebuyers on the overall homebuying process and also provides strategies for them to use with their personal finances. He truly cares for people and volunteers his time, money, and skills to ensure that everyone can learn something to assist them with reaching their full potential.

Joe is passionate about helping others. He volunteers to teach young adults with leading Home Buying & Wealth Building Cohorts geared toward those who desire to buy homes and learn financial strategies to better their financial standing. His work clearly shows that Joe has a heart for people, and this book is just one way that he attempts to assist, encourage, and motivate as many people as he can.

In *Generational Wealth Builder,* you'll find simple, easy-to-read guidance presented in a manner that readers can easily adopt in their everyday life. The book has three sections: Personal Finance, Succeeding at Life, and Home Buying & Wealth Building. There is an additional section written for active-duty military personnel and veterans.

In the Personal Finance section, basic budgeting is an important chapter for people to implement. A budget will keep you on track, allow you to build your savings, and enable you to reach future goals. I'd refer to it as a roadmap securing you financial future. Succeeding at Life provides basic guidance, from making educational choices to even supporting a cause you believe in. Again, practical guidance that will allow you to reach your full potential.

The Home Buying & Wealth Building section covers everything from inheritance to credit scores. This section contains guidance for buying a home and increasing net worth.

I ask you, the reader, to not only enjoy the book but also implement the strategies presented to benefit you and others to become a *Generational Wealth Builder.*

TABLE OF CONTENTS

PERSONAL

FINANCE

1

MANY AREN'T TAUGHT ABOUT FINANCES

The fact many families do not adequately discuss finances is a mystery. For some, they were not properly taught and simply don't know anything about managing finances. While this may contribute to the lack of proper understanding, it cannot be an excuse due to all of the information readily available through social media, the Internet, and books. As long as you have a desire to do better, you can. From research with friends, family, and clients, it was discovered that when finances are discussed, they often do not address the entire spectrum of roles money really plays and will play in the future. From being independent and single to having a family, preparing and maintaining personal finances is a crucial task for everyone and determines how you, your family, and those around you will live in the future.

Parenting is an important responsibility, and the goal should be to raise children to a point where they are able to take care of themselves. This is a huge undertaking and includes teaching skills like walking, talking, eating, bathing, dressing, reading, writing, exercising discipline and self-control, and showing respect. The list goes on and on since the parenting responsibility never ends; however, one important task parents often leave out is teaching about the value of money. The value of money is not going to the store and handing the clerk money or a credit card. **Children must be taught how to properly manage money**. I'll use my dad to explain how he taught me the "true value" of money.

When I was eleven or twelve, my father and I had a discussion about my clothing. I must explain to everyone that after my mother passed away, my father was my best friend. He took excellent care of me. He would have my clothes ironed and laid out for me the night before I went to school, and he would make sure my breakfast was ready in the morning. One day something changed the way he did business, and I don't think either one of us knew the long-term impact of what happened.

My father set my clothes out one night, and when I was getting dressed the next morning, I noticed my socks were stretched out, and I complained to my dad. One conversation led to another, and we came to a perfect fix. My dad stated that from that day on I would have to get my clothes out myself. He also decided to give me the social security check I had been receiving since my mother passed away. Here were his guidelines: 1) Put at least 10 percent in the church offering; 2) put money in my savings account; 3) purchase my own clothing and school supplies; and 4) pay for my own lunch at school. Some may say this was a lot to place on a child, and I agree! I appreciate the lesson he taught me. In high school, I had over one thousand dollars in my savings account, paid for my own car insurance (my dad agreed to pay my car note), and I even made a few small loans to my dad (interest free, of course). The point of the story is my dad taught me financial responsibility without explaining exactly how to save money. He set guidelines I had to follow, and this has made a true difference in my life. Thanks, Dad! One other note is that I was able to start my own business at the age of fourteen. It was incorporated in Arkansas, and the intent was to produce and market clowns. My business partner was my close relative, Treshia Green, a mother figure. I am extremely grateful that she encouraged me to try, even when nothing seemed to go the way we desired. Even though no money was ever earned from the business, I learned so much. One important fact I learned was that I could do anything I set my mind to. Can you imagine an eighth-grade student meeting with attorneys to incorporate a business? Parents, do not limit your children. If they have dreams and desires, encourage them. You never know what they will come up with.

Some may ask, "What exactly do I need to know that I do not already know?" My answer is you can always learn something from someone, whether it is a different perspective, a new way to accomplish something, or even what not to do. This book is for those who realize they can do better. Maybe you are not where you desire to be financially, and this book can help you develop sound habits to increase your net worth. Many listen to the wrong people. When we are trying to accomplish something, we often become discouraged by listening to family, friends, and other associates who are not attempting to better their financial standing. They may say they wouldn't do what you're trying to do, or they may not believe it will work. You should ask them to show you their financial statements. Many of them will probably get that "deer in headlights" look on their face. **If you want to achieve anything in life or become financially independent, you have to be willing to change your lifestyle, become educated in financial matters and, most importantly, associate with people who are where you are trying to go**. One example I will share is the fact I had and still have a strong desire to own a motor coach business. I have had a strong passion for buses since an early age. I actually wrote a business plan to start a nationwide bus company around the age of twelve. My plan included the equipment and land needed to successfully operate the business.

After I became an Air Force officer, I was given an assignment to Scott Air Force Base, Illinois, and met Pastors Eugene and Linda Connor. Pastor Eugene Connor just so happened to have charter buses. Well, you can see where this story is headed. Yes, my wife and I purchased a 1985 MCI 96A3 (forty-seven passenger forty foot long motor coach). I learned how to drive the bus and manage the affairs of owning a charter bus business. One major point I learned was that owning a bus was not as affordable as I had planned. The older equipment was difficult to maintain, and more money was required for maintenance than for a newer bus. On the other hand, a newer bus would have forced me to have a bus payment equivalent to my Air Force salary. That was not feasible! Pastor Connor taught me a lot spiritually, financially, and emotionally. I'm not taking anything away from my dad or my wife's parents, but sometimes someone from the outside can have a great impact on your life because you are more apt to listen to them.

In this day and age, it is easy for many people to claim to be experts in areas without being certified or even having the necessary experience to demonstrate how they can help you become successful. With so many people providing information and so many avenues for voices to be heard, it can be difficult to distinguish who you should listen to. If you are not a financial expert, this book will explain personal finance to you in a basic manner to make sure you understand. While finances are discussed, the book also explains how to actually get the most out of life. **Remember, even the smartest person can learn something from someone else**.

The road to financial freedom is not one that will allow you to purchase everything your heart desires all of the time. It will take sacrifice after sacrifice to travel the path to financial freedom and build a good foundation. **A good foundation is essential to having a life of financial independence and charting a path that will allow you to have options most people do not. It is easier to make more money when you have money**. Everyone knows the saying, "It takes money to make money." This is a true statement;

yet many people are not willing to save and invest to increase the amount of money they have. "It doesn't take money to get into debt." Think about that saying. People that don't have money tend to get into more debt. According to books I have read, many people who earned or saved substantial amounts of money in one generation have done so by being frugal. Despite having large sums of money, they still spend in the same frugal manner that enabled them to get where they are.

No matter what your age, background, career, or net worth, this book will explore areas you may not have thought about before. For men, it is intended to strengthen our role as brothers, sons, husbands, and fathers. For women, my hope is that it will help strengthen your knowledge to assist you in being better sisters, daughters, wives, and mothers. With the information provided, all who read this book will be able to build stronger, more financially stable budgets. This book will supplement other financial books you may already have and make bold statements that other people may not want to make. I personally challenge each and every person who reads this book to make a personal commitment to become better stewards over what you are blessed with. If our parents, grandparents, and great-grandparents had the opportunities available to us today, our family net worth may be greater than it is now. **Since we can't go back in time, it's up to us to build wealth and teach our family and others how to maintain it**. Now that we have covered these areas, here's to uncovering new paths and ways to developing a stronger financial foundation. Caution—the next chapter may be "Tough"!

TOUGH
FINANCIAL
LOVE

Many parents attempt to provide their children with everything they want; however, doing that will not level the playing field. The playing field is leveled by providing knowledge and wisdom they can take with them for the rest of their lives. My father understood this principle very well and was determined to teach me "Tough Financial Love."

My father was very strict and taught finances the hard way. He made me earn and pay for the things I wanted. As a child, going through his financial lessons, I wondered why he was so hard on me. As mentioned in chapter 1, around the age of twelve, we had a conversation that changed how both of us did business. I learned to save money and to seldom spend on wants. My father taught financial responsibility without explaining exactly how to save money. He set guidelines to follow, and this has made a true difference in my life.

A second example of tough financial love is that my father and I signed a contract that stated if I graduated in the top 10 in my high school class, he would provide $19,500 upon graduation. He was generous and offered to pay a $500 bonus if I graduated in the top 5. I ended up thirteenth out of more than 130 students, and my father, demonstrating tough financial love, congratulated me on my accomplishment and waved when I departed for the Air Force. I learned a valuable financial lesson. My father (just like society) does not reward the person who almost made it. Maybe I should have asked for a recount or prolonged the final decision somehow to see if he would change his mind! To be honest, it would not have mattered. Those who know my dad know that he stands on his word and does not change. Yes, even more than twenty years after high school graduation, this is still a sore subject for me. I was so close! I wasn't even given $15,000 . . . $10,000 . . . $5,000 . . . This was so frustrating! **I tried so hard; however, I could have done better**. There were some assignments I could have focused more on. I could have done better on some tests as well.

Parents, it is never too early to teach your children financial responsibility. Whether you provide an allowance or utilize other methods, the importance of money must be taught. As children mature into their teenage years, grade yourself. Would you trust them with your checkbook? If not, determine which areas of financial skill you need to help them improve in. If we do not properly teach our children, who will? By providing proper financial instruction, they will be on the path to financial independence. For this reason, we should provide "Tough Financial Love" while teaching them three important areas discussed in the next chapter that, if followed, will propel their finances to the next level.

$

PAY CHARITY,
PAY YOURSELF, AND
PAY YOUR BILLS

This is an important chapter. In order to become financially successful, it is important to implement three principles that include giving, investing in yourself, and ensuring you pay your debt obligations. The order identified is equally important.

Many successful people are philanthropists. Some donate to religious organizations, allowing them to build schools, feed the homeless, etc. This is often one of the more widely known and popular ways of giving. I advise that even when giving to religious organizations to make sure they have a true mission program. If the money is primarily used for overhead costs, you may have to ask yourself if this form of giving is truly aligned with your purpose. If there are outreach programs in place, your donations can reach the people who need it and truly be used according to the intended purpose.

While donating to a religious organization is a great way to give back, there are other non-profit organizations that are active in the community that also should be considered. Organizations that help the homeless and less fortunate while maintaining low overhead costs are excellent sources of support for your community. Sometimes these organizations have better outreach programs than religious ones! Donating to charity is a must. **The point of this section is not to tell you where to give but just to make sure that you give!** The "Rule of Giving" is important for us to understand, and the sooner we learn it, the sooner blessings are poured upon our lives. After this happens, you are ready for the next step.

Paying yourself is crucial. **Many people spend their whole life paying other people**. Don't get me wrong: I'm a firm advocate of paying your bills on time, but you have to pay yourself as well. By paying yourself, you are able to put money away for the future. I've heard young people say, "I may not be here tomorrow, so why should I save?" I have heard middle-aged people repeatedly say, "I wish I had invested and saved my money instead of spending it." There is a balance that has to be made. You can enjoy life every day, but that does not mean you have to wear the most expensive clothes and drive the most expensive car when your income is telling you to be more economical. **If you cannot be happy with yourself and what you presently have, money will not make you happy either**.

You must lay a proper foundation for yourself and your family in order to enjoy life to its fullest. I'm not saying you have to be rich to enjoy life, but if your family is in need or wants something, it is nice to be able to pay for it and not worry about where the money is coming from or if should have spent your money differently.

Let me address the importance of a financial foundation. According to the *Webster's II New College Dictionary*, the second definition of the word "foundation" is "the basis on which a thing stands, is founded, or is supported." The King James Version of the Bible talks about the importance of having a foundation in Matthew 7:24–27. It reads as follows:

Therefore whosoever heareth these sayings of mine, and doeth them, I will like him unto a wise man, which built his house upon a rock: And the rain descended, and the floods came, and the winds blew, and beat upon that house; and it fell not; for it was founded upon a rock. And every one that heareth these sayings of mine, and doeth them not, shall be likened unto a foolish man, which built his house upon the sand: And the rain descended, and the floods came, and the winds blew, and beat upon that house; and it fell: and great was the fall of it.

Before I make anyone upset, I must say that I am a firm believer in the Bible. If you are not a Christian believer, I am not attempting to convert or insult you. Even if you don't believe in the Bible, you can take these four scripture verses and use them as a basis for how to build your finances. In this part of the Bible, it was referring to a spiritual foundation, but if we look at it in a natural manner, we can use this for our finances as well. First of all, a wise man builds his house upon a rock . . . A rock is a solid structure that will stand the test of time. As described, when the rain fell, floods came, and the winds blew, the house did not fall. The rock that you need to build your foundation on is a combination of items. Some may view the foundation as only the cement structure a house or building sits on, but it is also the ground that supports the cement. You can have the strongest cement in the world, but if the ground beneath it begins to crumble, the foundation will also break apart. This is similar to the foolish man building his house on the sand. When the rain fell, floods came, and the winds blew, the house fell. The end of the verse specifically states that "great was the fall of it."

Now, let's go deeper. The financial foundation addressed in this book is not just your savings account. It consists of all the ground beneath you to include: an emergency fund, life insurance, disability insurance, short-term savings, mutual funds, IRAs, direct stock purchases, and any other investments that will aid in the long-term support of your family. Some investments may go down (mutual funds, stocks, etc.), but if you have all the investments you need, your overall foundation will withstand the storm. Be cautious of where you build your financial future. Your long-term success depends on it! Money can make your life easier by allowing you to buy the things you need and help you reach your dreams, but you must be happy without money to be truly happy with it. This is evident by looking at celebrities and professional athletes who have more money than many of us or our families will ever have but still have problems.

MAKE SURE YOU PAY YOUR BILLS ON TIME! Maybe I need to say this again . . . MAKE SURE YOU PAY YOUR BILLS ON TIME! I have been around people who never seem to get ahead. They have some nice things and spend big for Christmas, but after the holidays are over, the bills are piled on the table. They have to figure out what to pay in order to survive. Their credit is bad, and they have to pay high interest rates to get automobile financing and credit cards. They act like they are living large when in all actuality they are head over heels in debt. They repeat this process over and over and never get ahead. They live for today, but tomorrow they will still be paying for what they did yesterday, last year, and even years ago. They sink further and further into the black hole of debt. There is a way to stop this recessional pattern. The key word is **sacrifice**. If you want something bad enough, you will be willing to sacrifice things you want now to ensure you will be financially independent tomorrow. It will not be easy, but it will be worth it. You owe it to yourself, your spouse, your children, and other people you will cross paths with. If you come from a family similar to the one previously described, you can break the cycle. Don't suffer any longer than you have to. Now that you have come into the knowledge of this, use it to its full potential. I don't guarantee you will be wealthy or filthy rich in any certain period of time, but I do guarantee you will feel more confident and have fewer worries in life. It is worth it!

In order to get out of this pattern, you have to curb your spending. Make a conscious decision to pay all of your bills with your paycheck. There are some things necessary for survival, but curb your spending until you have credit card debt, automobiles, and other non-appreciating assets paid off. Once you are able to pay your bills and invest, you will then be able to have an allowance. **An allowance is not considered paying yourself . . . paying yourself involves investing for your future**. You have to PAY CHARITY, PAY YOURSELF, and PAY YOUR BILLS. Enough said.

4

YOU DRIVE A WHAT? HOW MUCH DO YOU MAKE?

Many people try to maintain a certain image either on social media or in-person. There are a lot of young people driving vehicles that are worth more than their parents, their grandparents, and their own net worth combined. This is a serious problem. Don't get me wrong, I'm a strong believer in having nice things. But you shouldn't overdo it. I see people with no vision for their future living a lifestyle that will destroy them and their families.

When a person buys a $30,000 to $40,000 vehicle or higher, how much money should they have or make per year? Realistically, many agree and teach that a car payment should be no more than 10 percent of your monthly net income. This is going to step on some people's toes, but this is wise counsel. You may be able to spend more, but as you read the following chapters, you'll get a good understanding why spending 10 percent or less of your monthly income on a car is recommended. Later in this chapter, another recommendation is made as to how you should pay for the vehicle you are attempting to purchase.

It is okay to enjoy the fruits of your labor and pamper yourself with the finer things in life as long as you have done everything that you need to do. When you are paying $600 or more a month and live with your parents or in a rented place, you are missing the point! There is nothing wrong with enjoying the finer things in life, but the finer things don't always cost the most. The bad thing about this is that people are promoting this faddish lifestyle. We are producing people who believe going into debt long term for depreciating assets is the way to go. In general, the people driving vehicles that aren't the newest, don't look the best, and are paid off are the ones who have it right. These people are the ones who have nice houses to go home to. These are the ones who don't have to have the latest vehicle that just came out. They don't have to have the latest outfit before others have it. These are the people you see in the grocery store with coupons. Yeah, you thought they were pinching pennies because they had to. Well, they do have to. They have required this of themselves because a penny saved is a penny earned. These are the same people who probably have a net worth closer to a million dollars than the ones who think spending a large portion of their money on vehicles means they have "made it."

Let's dissect a few things before we move to the next chapter. We have identified that people that look wealthy may be the ones with actually no wealth at all, and the ones that pinch pennies and don't have the latest gadgets are probably those with a positive net worth, money in their savings accounts, no or little credit card debt, and take vacations (not trips). Additional books I recommend are *The Millionaire Next Door* and *The Millionaire Mind*. Remember, if you want to become wealthy, you have to think like a wealthy person. A person making $1,500 a month while driving a vehicle that costs over $40,000 with seven-year financing may not see a problem with their situation, but it will hinder them from being financially independent and establishing a solid net worth. I can say it because even though I wasn't as bad as this scenario, I did have a car payment of $500 a month when my monthly income was $1,500. Despite having a high car payment compared to my monthly income, I made sure I donated to charity and placed $140 a month in a savings account. I sacrificed to purchase the vehicle I wanted (1997 Toyota Avalon XL—brand new). Later, I bought a used 1996 Toyota Avalon XLS that I purchased in 1998 after trading in the newer Avalon. I drove that car for over ten years and departed with it once the engine developed a major issue. The money I saved once the car was paid off was used for investing. My philosophy is that I don't plan to work my whole life to pay for temporary pleasure. If I sacrifice temporary pleasure, my investments will pay me the majority of my life.

When you are searching for a new or used car, you need to know how much vehicle you can afford. This is important, and if you don't know this, the dealer will attempt to place you in a vehicle they think you should be in. They'll put you in the most expensive car with a high interest rate, and you'll be on a quick path to destruction. In order to provide a quick reference tool for you to find how much of a car payment you can actually afford, here's a simple rule to follow. The car you can reasonably afford is the amount of money you can pay monthly for a car payment multiplied by twenty-four months. Here's the formula:

24 months times the amount of monthly payment you can reasonably afford per month.

For example, if you can afford to pay $500 maximum per month, you can afford a $12,000 car (24 x $500 = $12,000). As a reminder, we said above that an ideal monthly payment is 10 percent of your monthly net income. One fact you have to understand is that you can probably pay more than the $12,000 for the vehicle, but this formula is intended to keep you on the path to financial freedom. If the car you want is $20,000, you need to save $8,000 for a down payment before going to purchase the vehicle. Please understand the point I'm attempting to make. You may be able to afford a new luxury car, but your budget may be better suited to a more economical vehicle to align more with your goals and investments. This is only a guide to aid you in establishing a solid financial foundation. One fact I must point out is that most companies have special finance rates for individuals that have good credit and finance a vehicle with them. You should realize that I'm actually giving people a break by stating you can finance a car! Some say you shouldn't finance a car at all. I agree with them; however, I'm only providing a way for people to finance their purchase while incurring little or no finance charge and still remaining on the path to financial freedom.

The recommendations I have made are for personal vehicles. If you are a business owner purchasing a vehicle or equipment that will provide income to your company, the recommendation doesn't necessarily apply to you. At times, larger vehicles may be required due to the work you perform and having to transport people to different locations. The vehicles my recommendation concerns are vehicles that will cost you money and not provide any income to support them. If you really love cars and can't do without having the most expensive one on the highway, you may need to become an automobile dealer. By doing this, you can drive the car you like and sell them for a profit. There are state regulations you have to follow, but this can be a business that will provide great success to the car enthusiast. For additional information about pursuing this career, research your state requirements and contact local used car dealers in your area.

This chapter mainly addresses automobiles, but some thought should also be given to the clothing we wear. Some dress like they are millionaires when they are not even thousandaires. I'm not saying to let yourself go and wear clothing that does not help you look your best; however, if your wardrobe is worth more than your bank account and investments, you have your priorities in the wrong place. The clothing will either wear out, or you will eventually not be able to fit into it anymore, and if clothing is high on your list of spending priorities, your finances will be in trouble (if you aren't already there). There are nice articles of clothing that can be purchased on sale or at discount retailers. Some of them may not be suitable for whatever reasons, so you may choose to only procure the name-brand or high-dollar item. I understand this. Just make sure that you decrease your amount of spending as much as possible. Later on, you will be glad you did.

In the next chapter, we'll address if what you bought is really a financial blessing or a financial curse.

FINANCIAL BLESSING OR FINANCIAL CURSE

Today's generation desires to have everything instantly. We desire to "get rich quick" and want to "name and claim" our blessings. We are often excited about things we should be thankful for but that should not be the highlight of our lives. Getting a new car is a major milestone for people just beginning to make it on their own. They should be proud of the fact they have "grown up" and made a big purchase independently. But is the purchase, in reality, a financial blessing or a financial curse?

I have seen many people spend lavishly with nothing really to show for it. I have seen the young get older with nothing to really show for it. What is the impact of poor financial decision-making on our lives? Improper planning causes us to start online fundraising campaigns to pay for expenses we should normally have been able to cover. Improper planning makes life more difficult to handle financial challenges. This can be avoided! You do not have to make the most amount of money to plan. No matter how much or how little you make, a plan will assist you and guide you to your goal.

The Bible states in Proverbs 10:22, "The blessing of the Lord, it maketh rich, and he addeth no sorrow with it." This means that if you receive something you think is a blessing, it should not add any sadness with it. If a new car is harming your budget, or if it is causing problems within your marriage, you must decide if it is really a blessing or a curse. While we must have transportation, it doesn't mean we have to spend too much of our income on a vehicle when a less expensive one will also work.

I will confess that I purchased a vehicle that was well within 10 percent of my net income. According to the numbers, I had no problem paying for it; however, I felt convicted that I was paying that much money for a vehicle (one that I *really* liked). Again, the numbers showed that I could afford it, and I had an extremely low interest rate. I ended up trading the vehicle in and purchasing a less expensive one. While this is a vehicle example, we must look at all of our spending habits to make sure we are not bringing down a financial curse on our family. Just because we have the money to spend on an something does not mean we can really afford to buy it.

While we all work hard and tell ourselves that we deserve certain things, we must realize it is not about us. There is a much larger picture we need to see. It is ultimately about our families. Are we really witnessing financial blessings when people are going further in debt and our communities continue to struggle? Is it a financial blessing to have bad credit but get financed at a 30 percent interest rate for a car? Is it a curse to drive an old car that is paid for? Our society often has things mixed up. We believe that having the most things will show that you are blessed, and we fail to realize the massive amount of debt that goes along with the things. Look over your financial situation and then keep the financial blessings and eliminate the financial curses.

It is never too late to make a change. If your finances need a little help because you are not going in the right direction, now is the time to make corrective steps. You can start with a minor adjustment, but the main point is to at least start. Without taking proper corrective actions, you may exhibit Roller Coaster Finances in the future.

ROLLER COASTER
FINANCES

This financial topic was given to me while Pastor Andrew Jackson Jr. from West Irving Church of God in Christ in Irving, Texas, was preaching. He mentioned that Christians' spiritual walk should not be a roller coaster. We should not be happy one moment then sad the next minute. Despite going through trials, we should remain strong, determined, and committed to being an example for others to follow. The same principle can be stated from a financial standpoint.

Financially speaking, we all should have a solid budget and money set aside for emergency situations. By living within our means and not trying to impress others, we can live a comfortable lifestyle and be content where we are. If something unexpectedly happens, we will be in a position to confront the challenge and not worry about how to deal with it.

Many people love the thrill of roller coasters and enjoy conquering the largest and fastest rides available at amusement parks. The suspense of the roller coaster inching slowly toward the first drop excites and terrifies people at the same time. When the coaster drops, it builds up speed and zooms left, right, up, down, upside down, and through all the twists and turns the engineers designed. At the end of the ride, the coaster stops and lets its participants off. People smile and discuss their experience while they move on to the next ride. While the roller coaster ride is highly desired for thrill seekers, finances should not exhibit roller coaster qualities.

An example of roller coaster finances is when a person receives income but forgets to pay a bill. Happy to get their paycheck, they rush out to go shopping and later enjoy a night on the town, but the happiness quickly vanishes when the forgotten bill arrives and they find themselves coming up short. While life is often filled with many ups and downs, we should strive to have our finances steadily climb the track instead of being turned upside down, inside out, and twisting until nothing else is left. Pastor Jackson often states that people can't even *find* the ends, so they definitely can't make the ends meet! This is a problem many face but that can be corrected by consistently keeping finances off the roller coaster track.

The best way to get your finances off the roller coaster is to create and live by a budget. You must track your spending on a monthly and yearly basis, and your overall debt should be a key component as well. Monitoring where you are today will provide motivation to get you to a better place tomorrow. Stay encouraged and be disciplined, and you can get off that financial roller coaster.

7

BASIC BUDGETING

Following a budget is the equivalent of following a highway to get to your destination. Sure, you can get where you want to go by driving off-road instead of the highway, but it will be far more difficult—and you may not make it at all. You do not need an elaborate, fancy budget sheet to help you. A simple Excel file or even notes on a sheet of paper can assist you. The longer you use a budget, the more you can tailor it to what really works for you.

At a minimum, a budget should show your income, bills, and amount of money remaining after using your income to pay your bills. This will serve as a quick-reference way to document how much money you have left after paying your bills or if something needs to be adjusted due to having an income shortfall. I also recommend identifying your total assets and liabilities in order to show your net worth. Your real estate, money in the bank, investments, etc., are your assets. Your liabilities are what you owe, and it is possible for an asset to also be a liability. For example, if you own a home that is worth $200K, it is an asset, and this amount will be in the asset area. If you still owe $100K on the home, this will go in the liability section since it is a debt you still owe. The difference between the two items is your net worth (for this particular item) and would be $100K ($200K–$100K). You would do the same scenario for all of major component of your net worth. Some items will not be an asset at all. Any credit card debt will only be listed under the liability area and reduce the overall net worth depending on the amount of credit card debt you have. Using the previous example, if you have $10K in credit card debt, your $100K in net worth would now be reduced to $90K ($100K–$10K).

A true budget will tell you the truth about your finances, where you stand, and where you need to go. One time, I completed a budget for someone, and they literally cried because they did not know how bad their situation really was. They made nice money; however, they spent the majority of it. This is why a budget is critical for everyone—no matter how much or how little you earn.

Your budget can also be a tool to show trends you may have to deal with. It can show how much money you spend on utilities during certain times of the year to allow you to budget accordingly in the future. It can also be used as a tool to analyze the impact of a pay raise, a pay cut, or even of leaving your job to start a business. By knowing how much money you need to live, you can make proper decisions to positively impact your finances.

To Save or Not to Save

An email was received from a reader of a magazine I used to write for asking what to do about her financial situation. Specifically, she asked what she should do with a sizeable amount of money in a savings account. Due to her situation, the recommendation was for her to leave the money in a savings account instead of placing the money in a potential higher earning investment account. Instead of focusing on saving, she should focus on the immediate situation she was facing. I am certain that she is one of many people who have asked or will ask, do I save money, or do I not save at all? The answer is—it depends.

Saving for retirement is a must; however, we all need to take a good look at our individual situation and make sure we don't take the approach that one size fits all. Previously, many were told to put as much money as possible into investment accounts without considering their overall financial situation. If you have massive amounts of credit card, student loan, car, and mortgage debt, it may be more advantageous for you to pay the debt off before beginning an aggressive long-term investment plan.

Despite your debt amount, there is one situation where it is to your advantage to invest. For employer-sponsored savings plans with company matching contributions, you should at least contribute the minimum amount required to obtain the maximum matching contributions. For example, if your employer provides a 7 percent match of your income when you contribute 6 percent of your income, this is free money, and you need to take it by investing what is required to obtain the contribution. If your employer does not provide a match to your contribution, it may be more beneficial for you to pay your debt off. Remember that paying off debt does not "entitle" you to obtain additional debt.

One important long-term goal is to have your home paid for prior to your retirement, and it is important to factor in additional payments if necessary to achieve this goal. While thirty-year mortgages allow you to have a lower payment compared to shorter mortgage terms, you need to adequately plan to ensure you can enjoy retirement without a mortgage. You will still be responsible for taxes and insurance, but owning the home without a mortgage payment reduces some of the financial need during your retirement years. Besides paying the mortgage completely off, you also need to have enough income to last in your retirement years. You should establish "streams of income" that will last a lifetime through retirement savings; these income streams might come from a business you create or a part-time hobby. To save or not to save varies for everyone depending on specific situations, and while you may be in a period where you should not save, once the period passes, you should continue your plan to ensure you have a prosperous financial future.

Importance of a Good Credit Score

Your credit score is your financial report card. Those with excellent credit demonstrate a strong ability to pay their debt obligations on time and manage their overall amount of debt relative to their income. When you first start applying for credit, the issue faced will be the lack of a credit history. This lack of credit history can be similar to having challenging credit; however, there are some ways to develop a solid credit history.

One way that assists with developing a solid credit history is being added as a "signer" on the account of someone who already has strong credit. For example, a parent may add a child to a credit card; however, while the child may be included, I would not recommend providing them a credit card. Over time, the credit history from the credit card will be included on the child's report, and as long as the payments are made on time, this will assist the child to develop a positive credit history with minimal impact to anyone.

A second option is to obtain a secured credit card with a low credit limit that can be used for small purchases and paid back. For example, obtaining a secured credit card with a $300 limit would require $300 deposited with the bank, but when you get a bill, you would pay it with your current funds (and not with the amount that is securing the card at the bank). Once your credit history begins to build, you may be able to obtain a traditional unsecured credit card. Be advised that credit card debt is not good and I am not promoting it; however, using credit wisely and using the card based on how much cash you have to pay it off is wise because you will be developing good credit, and this will pay off big-time in the future. This action will prevent financial hardship, provide higher credit scores, and establish excellent credit utilization habits.

Credit utilization is very important. Many financial professionals state that credit card utilization should be 30 percent or lower. If you have a $10,000 credit card limit, your credit card balance should not be more than $3,000. While credit card debt should not be kept, the credit agencies monitor the credit utilization and deem that usage over 30 percent means you are living off your credit cards.

If needed, a parent may also cosign for a loan with a child. This is very risky, but parents should know their children. If they feel cosigning will help their child, they may find the decision worth it. While this option is definitely not recommended, it can still be used if needed. Cosigning is not recommended when the strong borrower is looking to make major financial changes such as buying a home.

Besides building new credit, there are also areas where people need to improve their existing credit score due to derogatory, delinquent, or poor credit choices that negatively impact their score. The most important way to improve your credit score in these scenarios is to pay your bills on time. While companies may promote ways to magically make the negative reporting disappear from your history, the best approach is to show companies that you are now paying your debt obligations on time. One way to prevent negative credit history is to always be prepared for financial challenges.

PREPARING FOR FINANCIAL CHALLENGES

Has your paycheck not been enough for you to make it through the month, week, or even the day? While the cost of living is steadily rising, our pay has seemed to remain the same or even decrease. There are many financial challenges we all face, and the way we prepare for the challenges will determine how well we can recover. Typically, I playfully refer to this as the Finance Demon that goes house to house trying to interrupt our plans. While the demon may not carry a pitchfork or have horns on his head, his financial attack is serious and can lead to financial destruction. The demon throws unplanned expenses our way to get our mind away from saving and preparing for the future. The Finance Demon has also tricked us into believing that we should measure our self-worth by what we have. He places a Spending Spirit inside of us and convinces us to do whatever it takes to acquire more things even if we pay more for them than what they are worth.

Payday Loans: If I pay it back, everything will be okay, right?

Some people turn to payday lending companies when faced with financial struggles or when they desire to buy things they can't afford. These companies advertise catchy slogans and provide a "band-aid" relief to an immediate financial problem, but using their services can place you in a worse situation than before you walked in their door. Payday lending companies are heavily represented in less affluent areas and increase the financial struggle for those who struggle the most. Normal interest rates for an unsecured personal loan through banks and credit unions may range from 5 percent to 20 percent depending on your credit history. While some of these rates are high, payday lending companies often charge 100 percent to even 300 percent or more for borrowing money for a short time. Imagine that you are broke month after month after month without using a payday lending company. Now . . . you happen to take out a payday loan one time and are charged 300 percent interest! If you couldn't make it previously, how will paying back 300 percent worth of interest correct your financial situation? While situations can and do happen, sometimes our money troubles start because we just want to have more than we need.

How to fix it: Resist the Finance Demon and it will flee!

Mark 3:27 states: "No man can enter into a strong man's house, and spoil his goods, except he will first bind the strong man; and then he will spoil his house." It is time for our strong men and women to not be bound any more. Resist the Finance Demon as well as the urge to cater to the Spending Spirit, and they will flee!

Breaking the spending habit can be difficult. With holidays, birthdays, and other special occasions, there is always a reason to overspend. It is at these moments that you have to stand your ground and not budge. Know that by protecting your budget and finances, you will emerge in a better situation. Stay strong . . . financial sacrifice will greatly help to increase your financial well-being.

FINANCIAL
SACRIFICE

People are taught to work hard and get a good education but are not properly instructed about all the roles money plays and will play in their future. Whether you are a college graduate embarking on your career or an established professional, you have learned how to sacrifice your time, but too often financial sacrifice is not understood and not actually made. Financial sacrifice along with a vision for the future will allow you to build wealth and ensure you can pass it on to future generations.

Many people think what you drive, how large your house is, and having a nice wardrobe define you. **Don't let others define who you are . . . define who you are to others!** If your friends drive BMWs but your budget allows for a Chevrolet, drive that Chevrolet with pride and a smile on your face. If you follow a financial plan, you may be able to pay cash one day for the BMW. While we should have nice things and enjoy what we work so hard for, we should do so in moderation to protect our financial future.

We previously recommended that a budget is a necessity for building and maintaining a strong financial foundation. If you are not using a budget, create one immediately to track your finances and guide your spending habits. The budget should outline your income, expenditures, and investments and also document your debt balances. Following a budget keeps you on the correct path and allows you to see the facts concerning your finances. By eliminating spending on wants, money will be available to pay off debt. Whether you have a mortgage, car loan, student loan, or credit card, now is the time to eliminate debt.

If you do not have any money available after all bills are paid or do not have enough to pay your bills, immediate action is needed! Spending more than you are earning must be stopped because it will bring catastrophe. Depending on the circumstances, extreme measures may need to be taken. Economic times are challenging for many in our nation, but if you develop a plan and do not give up, you can improve your financial situation by making your income go further while reducing your spending. Everyone's plan is different; however, the end result should be the same and will involve sacrifice.

From a financial standpoint, sacrifice enables you to develop a solid financial foundation and build wealth. Many people live for today without planning for tomorrow, and the lack of planning forces them to pay for previous purchases for years to come. There is a way to stop this recessional pattern, and the key word is sacrifice. Developing a strong desire to eliminate debt and sacrificing the things you want today will ensure financial independence tomorrow. While the road may not be easy, it is an important one to travel . . . and the trip will be worth it! Your financial sacrifice will be like trying to lose the extra pounds some of us struggle to take off. Similar to how unwanted fat creates challenges and even long-term health issues, we must trim the financial fat to ensure a happy financial future.

$

10

TRIM THE FINANCIAL FAT

The New Year often begins with people setting goals to exercise more and lose weight. From a financial standpoint, "fat" prevents you from maintaining wealth and reaching your goals. Naturally, it can be a challenge to get rid of a few extra pounds, and it may seem like the harder you exercise, the harder your body fights your attempt to lose weight. Unnecessary spending can be just as difficult as fat to eliminate. Just like fat damages our bodies with cholesterol, high blood pressure, and other diseases, financial fat will damage our ability to build wealth for years to come.

Financial fat can come from internal and external challenges that affect your ability to maintain wealth. Internal challenges include our natural tendencies to get frustrated and not see the progress we are actually making. An example is paying off a car loan; instead of using the extra money to pay down the loan, the money is used to purchase stuff we don't need. Having the will power to resist the urge to purchase unneeded things will strengthen your finances and allow you to maintain the wealth you are building. Whether you have $1 or $1,000,000, needless spending will leave you financially depleted. Everyone must develop a plan to maintain wealth no matter how little or much they have.

While you can control internal challenges, external challenges require "playing by the rules." External challenges include family members, friends, the Internal Revenue Service, and anyone or anything else with the ability to decrease your wealth. The government has rules and regulations everyone must follow to prevent their wealth from being confiscated. Federal, state, county, and city taxes must be paid to prevent you from losing your property or even spending time in jail. People of all walks of life confront issues with taxes, which can cause severe consequences for people and their families. Those who do not pay taxes on their property create great investment opportunities for others when properties with unpaid taxes are auctioned. Play by the rules . . . don't give your wealth away!

While it is definitely a blessing to give rather than to receive, giving your wealth away without taking care of yourself can be detrimental to your financial health. It's like flying. The flight attendant instructs you to put your oxygen mask on before you help someone else. The point is that if you don't take care of yourself, you will not be in a position to help anyone else. The same story applies to finances.

Any form of debt is considered financial fat. Debt is the cholesterol in our financial arteries. Without a budget, you may not know the debt is there, and it can silently kill you. While people claim there is good cholesterol and bad cholesterol, people also claim there is good debt and bad debt. Well, cholesterol is cholesterol, and debt is debt! You should get rid of both of them. Yes, a student loan and mortgage are good forms of debt, but a solid plan to pay them off early instead of in ten and thirty years respectively is a good idea. Any fat that attempts to destroy your financial future must be eliminated. Make a resolution to "trim the financial fat"!

$

11

YOUR PERSONAL FINANCIAL STRATEGY

Your personal financial strategy is one that you must develop and tailor to your individual needs. You can be as aggressive or conservative as you desire; however, our recommendation is that you at least be consistent. Despite what you were or were not taught about finances, you hold the key to your financial future. There are no excuses at this point! You control your financial destiny. You will have to find the tough financial love to help you reach the important goals before you.

When developing your financial strategy, it is recommended that you donate to charity, invest in yourself, and make sure you always pay your bills. It is crucial that as you budget, you follow the principles just mentioned. Not only will this allow you to help others, but it will allow you to always live off less money than you make. When you develop your budget, it may be tempting to spend extra money you are able to find. While this may provide short-term satisfaction, the best approach is to ward off additional financial curses on you and your family with sound financial planning. Sure, a new car may seem like a nice reward, but ask yourself if this would really be the best financial move for you.

With basic budgeting, you will be able to prepare for any financial challenges life throws at you. While others may seem to ride the financial roller coaster as a normal way of life, by exercising discipline and financial sacrifice, you will be on the path to financial freedom. Use your budget as your roadmap to guide you along the financial journey. At times, you may get off track, and that is okay. You will not be perfect! It is wise and responsible to at least recognize when you deviate from your financial plan in order to make immediate corrections. Remember, you should enjoy life, but enjoying life does not mean spending too much on material things.

I have made my share of financial mistakes. Some of them were costlier than others, but they allowed me to become who I am today. If I could do some things over, I would definitely have made some different financial decisions at times. My overall main piece of advice is to think before you make financial decisions. Ask yourself what the ten-year-older version of you say about this decision. Will the decision help or hurt your financial future?

At times you may feel that following the budget is too challenging and not rewarding. Stay strong! You can do this! You got this! Encourage yourself however you need to. Your financial future is depending on you to take control and place yourself in a strong position.

By implementing your financial strategy, you will normalize your savings, investing, and budgeting aspect of your life. You'll also eliminate debt by trimming the financial fat in your budget. All debt—student loans, car, credit cards, etc.—should be eliminated. Afterward, real estate should also be paid off early instead of taking the traditional thirty years. These steps will allow you to enjoy life and be on the path to being a Generational Wealth Builder.

Below are four points I recommend to assist with your financial strategy:

- ➜ Develop and utilize a budget
- ➜ Build and maintain an emergency fund
- ➜ Prepare for and invest in additional financial investment opportunities
- ➜ Motivate others to reach their full financial potential

EXAMPLE OF GOALS:

SHORT-TERM | LONG-TERM GOALS:

1. _____

2. _____

3. _____

4. _____

5. _____

6. _____

7. _____

$

Additional Page for Your Notes

SUCCEEDING
AT LIFE

WHAT YOUR PARENTS SHOULD HAVE TAUGHT YOU

As I said, my father taught me financial responsibility at an early age. I became frugal, savvy, financially conservative. I spent money on what I needed, but I regularly contributed to my savings account When my father once had to borrow from my savings, I got very upset because not even *I* took money from my savings account. These values and principles were instilled in me early on, and they have only deepened as I have matured. I don't claim to know it all, but I do know that if you have faith and try hard, all things are possible.

Life is not fair. You can be the most qualified person and not get the job. You can be the smartest person and not get selected for the opportunity. You can have the biggest heart and still be disappointed by others. Through all of your trials and situations, you must maintain an inner determination and drive. Do not allow anyone to take that from you.

It is normal to feel disappointed at times, but you must channel that negative energy in order to motivate yourself to do better. My disappointment consisted of wondering why my father didn't give me handouts—why he didn't buy me a new car upon high school graduation. I constantly watched him help others, but with his own son, there were no handouts. Did it make me upset, frustrated, disappointed, confused, etc? Yes, it sure did! I still cannot explain why he did certain things. Personally, I feel he was being cheap toward me; however, it all worked out for my good. That is the point that needs to be driven home here. Even when things do not work the way you believe they should, learn the lesson and move forward.

Parents should teach financial responsibility. Whether an allowance or some other method is used, the importance of money must be taught. When my daughter was three, she was already asking for money on a regular basis. Fortunately for me, one dollar worked well then; however, now . . . well, she's a little more expensive! We attempted to teach both of our children financial responsibility at an early age; but we still provide financial advice to them and plan to always do so (whether they listen or not).

Understand that your parents should treat you like the eagle treats its young. Yes, the eagle is a mighty bird when you see them grown, but you didn't see them as an eaglet. The eaglet's responsibility is to learn how to take care of themselves—to fly, hunt, and so on. The parent is so strict on their eaglets that they throw them out of the nest. They'll give them a few practice attempts, and if they can't fly, they'll swoop beneath them and save them from the fast-approaching ground. They only perform this "saving-method" a few times. You will not see an adult eagle still being rescued by their parent. We can learn a lot from the eagle.

Looking back, I noticed that some of my childhood peers didn't get the same hardcore training I did. Their parents constantly made sure they were in name-brand clothing, had money in their pockets, and never felt pressured to get good grades in school. At the time we were there, it seemed like they were really enjoying life, and looking back on it, maybe they were. But if the principles and responsibilities of saving and spending were not stressed, it is pretty likely that poor finances have had an impact on their quality of life. It is true that life is not fair, but parents cannot level the playing field by giving their children everything they want. The playing field is leveled by providing the knowledge and wisdom children can take with them. This knowledge and wisdom can be attained through financial literacy as well as educational opportunities.

13

EDUCATIONAL
CHOICES

Educational choices are abundant and oftentimes it is difficult for young and older students to decide what field of study to pursue. The focus of this chapter is geared toward high school students preparing for college life; however, it is for anyone trying to determine what major they should pursue.

Do you have a passion? Is there something you truly love to do? Is there something you would do for free because you enjoy learning about it so much? Personally, I love aviation. I remember telling the Air Force I would fly for free (as long as they gave my family a place to stay, and food). This is a field that I decided to study because no matter how much or little I made, I enjoyed working around airplanes.

College life is not going to be easy, so it is best to find a path that you will enjoy. If you have to sacrifice by spending time apart from family and friends, getting to study something you love will make the sacrifice a little less painful. Make sure the program you decide on is one *you* really enjoy. People can make recommendations, but at the end of the day, you are the one who will have to go to work each day. Pick a field you will enjoy!

Grades are important. . . Yes, grades are important, but not necessarily for the reason most think. When you apply for positions once you graduate, employers will rank you against other applicants based on the school, degree program, and your grades. It is important that you make good grades, but it is even more important that you learn! While grades carry weight, what matters more is that you allow your mind to grow and be stimulated.

The financial side of the degree is often not discussed, so I'll make some points worth remembering here. First of all, you should apply for as many scholarships as possible while in high school (and even when you are in college) to help offset as much of the financial liability for college tuition, books, and lodging as you can. A dollar saved is a dollar earned. Any dollar borrowed will cost you more than a dollar when you pay it back!

Pick your degree program wisely. It is not beneficial to accumulate a hundred thousand dollars in debt for a degree program that will only pay you thirty or forty thousand dollars a year. You must treat your degree program as an investment. Your investment should provide a nice return, or it may not be worth it. I have assisted many clients who have so much student loan debt that with their current income, they will not be able to pay it off in their lifetimes. This is not the way to go. Don't compromise your financial future because others insist you *have* to get a college degree.

Education is important because knowledge is power. Does everyone need a bachelor's, master's, or doctoral degree? I don't think so. There's nothing wrong with obtaining these types of degrees; however, vocational and technical programs that allow you to make a good living are options as well. There are welders working in the oil and gas field earning approximately a hundred thousand dollars (with overtime). This is a lot of money for someone who may not have a college degree.

Find your path and make your way along it in the most efficient manner possible. I entered the Air Force and utilized the Tuition Assistance program. My total student loan for my bachelor's degree was eight thousand dollars, and this was really for me to obtain my pilot's license. The overall return on investment for the cost of my degree was great. My degrees increased my knowledge and also expanded my entrepreneurial possibilities. Find your path, nurture it with good education, and keep the costs of your education to a minimum!

14

RESET YOUR PRESET

During one Sunday morning worship service at West Irving Church, Elder Jamaal Mellerson made a profound statement. He strongly proclaimed that we all need to "Reset Our Preset." He was referring to the spiritual realm, but this is also relevant to finances. Do you need the four-thousand square foot home with a three-car garage? Do you need to drive a $60,000 vehicle? Do you need to spend $1,000 eating out each month? Do you need to wear $200 tennis shoes? If you "Reset Your Preset," you will make correct financial decisions to put you on the path to financial freedom.

Many people today believe we are entitled to have the finest things in life. Just because you can afford a $500,000 home doesn't mean you have to spend that much. Even though you can finance a $60,000 vehicle, it may be wise to purchase a $30,000 one instead. We are programmed to spend money to demonstrate that we have finally "made it." The problem is . . . well, we haven't made it! Many times, those attempting to show everyone what they have are drowning in debt, and those content with who they are and what they have are better off financially.

Life might not always be fair, but life does offer us the opportunity to live our dreams. Money should be utilized to benefit both you and the entire community. Every action we take should be thoroughly thought through. For example, if companies do not treat you fairly, I believe you should not do business with them. Use wisdom and spend your hard-earned money wisely.

No matter who you are, you must have a place to live. Why pay others when you can have a home of your own? The decrease in home values has provided an opportunity for many who otherwise would have been left behind. In some instances, you will find that a mortgage payment will be close to what is being paid in rent. Home ownership can still help you build a solid foundation for you and your family.

Some may believe they are cursed due to their parents or even grandparents' mistakes, but we all have the power to change the future. Money is powerful! Instead of squandering it, I challenge you to save and invest your money. Show everyone that you are intelligent and powerful; grow your wealth instead of purchasing depreciating assets.

Your changed mind will benefit you and others you come in contact with. Make up your mind today . . . Reset Your Preset!

15

THE END OF
ENTITLEMENTS

There have been many discussions about how our government can no longer afford entitlement programs. Social Security, Medicare, and even veteran's programs are at risk of being reduced or eliminated. The funny thing is that the people at the top are trying to financially weaken those who helped propel them to their current financial heights. Let me be frank: no one makes money without taking it from someone else. The exchange of money is either voluntary or involuntary, but the money must be exchanged from one person to another.

We must take care of our responsibilities and not depend on others; however, the problem is that certain groups believe they are exempt from working. **[CAUTION: Reader discretion is advised.]** People at the top have become accustomed to receiving entitlements. An example is that our government officials can be unproductive, get very little work accomplished, and ultimately cripple our nation; however, they still get paid! When was the last time you were unproductive for months at your job and still received a paycheck? The system is different for those at the top. They are entitled to it, right?

Businesses pay their Chief Executive Officers (CEOs) and other leaders ridiculous amounts of money. While I do not believe the government should create laws limiting the salaries of CEOs, I believe we should be smart about what businesses we support with our money. CEOs feel they are entitled to very high salaries, and we as the consumer continue to support their excessive salaries by paying too much for their products. This entitlement needs an adjustment!

This is certainly true of government and business leaders, but our church leaders must also change the way they think. I make the caveat right at the outset in this section by saying I am a firm believer in following God's principles. I actively support charitable organizations and also give to people placed on my heart. I believe we need more church leaders with a pure heart and who have the people's best interest in mind. Pastor Andrew Jackson Jr. is a great example for others to follow. He is humble and will give his last to make sure church members are properly taken care of. The church family freely gives when he asks for something because his heart is clearly shown. With a leader like this, I will give my last to make sure he is taken care of.

On the opposite spectrum are leaders who are more concerned about their position and level of power than the people who helped propel them to their privileged positions. It is a touchy subject, but it is one that should be addressed. If success comes only at the expense of others, I don't want any part of it. Let's end entitlements—starting at the top first!

$

16

LOOKS CAN BE DECEIVING

Be careful when you compare yourself to others. You may see what they desire you to see and not the whole picture. With social media, it is easy to be misled by the image others project. There is nothing wrong with using social media, but when you compare yourself to what you see, it can easily throw you off course. Ask yourself how many pictures did someone take to get the "perfect" one? Do they show the good *and* the bad? Normally, people only show the best, and this does not mean that everything is going the way they desire or plan. It just means they are showing you what they want you to see.

When you see someone driving an expensive car, what is your first thought? Do you wish you had it? Do you wonder how much they are paying for it? Do you question how hard they had to work in order to purchase it? Many times, we simply look at the good without looking at the work involved.

You can also apply this to relationships. People may see a couple that has been married for twenty-plus years and wish their relationship was similar to that couple. There is nothing wrong with desiring to be better and seeing what others have, but you must understand that you may not see everything they went through to obtain their present happy condition. Looks can definitely be deceiving. Do not get caught up in looks, and do not get caught up in comparing yourself to others!

To be transparent, I have faced many disappointments in my life. From losing my mother when I was six years old to breast cancer to career obstacles. People may look at me and think I'm doing well—and I would have to say I think I am doing pretty well. But there have been many times where I was frustrated and questioned why things didn't work out the way I desired.

One of the biggest disappointments was being unable to fly for the Air Force. I checked all of the boxes and was even selected to become an Air Force pilot. No matter how hard I tried, top-level leadership would not provide the waiver I needed to allow me to pursue my dreams. It was heartbreaking. At one point, I was going to separate from the Air Force; however, one of my commanders provided mentoring and helped me overcome the situation. While my career still turned out well, there is still a void born of not getting to do something I was passionate about. When you see me now, you do not see the hurt I experienced. I channeled the hurt into positive energy that forced me to continue persevering regardless of what the situation looked like. It is okay to be disappointed. It is okay to be frustrated. It is okay to fail. I just want you to get up, dust yourself off, and keep moving forward!

17

MONEY VERSUS
HAPPINESS

Money plays an important part in our lives. We use it to pay for what we need and want. We work for money, save money, spend money, count money, and think about how to get more money. Those who do not have money often believe money can provide happiness; however, I'm here to tell you it can't.

If you had to choose between money and happiness, what would it be? Would you choose money without happiness or happiness without money? Can you be truly happy without money? Can you enjoy money without happiness?

If you cannot be happy without money, I guarantee that you will not be happy *with* money! If you can be happy when you are down to your last dime, once you are successful, you will be happy with money. If you are only happy when everything is going your way and you have money, your happiness may not be based on true internal satisfaction but on the money you have.

Should a person sacrifice their own happiness for others? Should you sacrifice your desires to make others happy? Can you make that sacrifice and not regret it? These are all internal questions you must address. My belief is that you should attempt to make others happy, especially those you truly love, and this may indeed involve sacrifice. But when you deny yourself for the sake of others, you will find that true happiness is more than just money.

But let's deal with the money side first. It is important that you have at least enough money to meet your needs and maybe some wants. Life would be boring if you could have everything you wanted. Some may disagree, but part of the fun of this thing we call life is working toward something and being able to reach it at last. You should not struggle your whole life, but with the struggle comes appreciation when you finally obtain success.

Let's assume for a moment that you have more money than you could ever imagine. You can have the nice home, expensive car, and travel to distant destinations on a private jet. The only catch is that you are doing all of this by yourself. Will you be happy? Let's assume you continue this for five, ten, or even fifteen years. Are you still happy? We are naturally wired to get a "charge" from others. A big hug or a tight squeeze can do so much for us.

Now, what if we remove the nice home, expensive car, and travel by private jet, but you now have friends and family who are 100-percent by your side. You have people who love you and who you love. No matter what you go through, they are there for you. You feel like you are on top of the world even though you have almost nothing by worldly standards. This can be categorized as true happiness.

We'll get back to finance now, but just remember that it means nothing to amass a fortune but wind up a lonely person in this world.

$

18

PREPARING FOR MARRIAGE

Marriage is a huge step for both people. They are each gaining a companion, friend, and a spouse. Men, we are responsible for ensuring our families are taken care of emotionally, spiritually and, yes, financially. I recommend that anyone preparing for marriage or already married read a personal favorite book of mine titled *Resolving Conflict in Marriage* by Bishop Darrell L. Hines. You'll find it stimulating and very easy to understand. There is also a detailed chapter on finances. Take my word for it: this is a must-have in your library to share with your significant other.

If you can't remember anything from this book, please take heed of this section. When you are looking for a spouse or preparing for marriage, make sure the person you are dating sees things similar to the way you do. Since this book deals with finances, let's strictly deal with seeing finances as a financial conservative versus as a heavy spender. The Bible says in Proverbs 18:22, "Whoso findeth a wife findeth a good thing, and obtaineth favour of the Lord." All too often men don't find her, but, all too often men are not what the woman needs either. Yes, I said it. Women can't point fingers at men, and men can't point fingers at women. Both sides have work to do to ensure their spouses will not be disappointed. The next paragraph is for the men . . .

We need to get this right. While you are single, you can make due with ramen noodles and cereal if you have to. I know some people who have very nice clothes and cars but don't have any meat in the refrigerator. As a man, this shows we know how to sacrifice, but we need to sacrifice for other things too. I guarantee you that if you are married and don't have any food in the refrigerator, but you're driving an expensive vehicle with rims, your wife will be rightfully upset and you will not have peace in your home. Here's a quick note: when you become married, you will have to sacrifice things you want in order to make sure your spouse is happy. If she's happy, you'll be happy (I hope you understand that). A woman wants security. She wants a man who can provide a nice house, food, clothes, and transportation. If your vehicle payment is too high, you need to reevaluate your financial situation. Prepare to change immediately. This example may be extreme, but I only want to drive home the point that you may have to make changes to your lifestyle before you get married. Marriage will force you to change, but it is easier to change before marriage than after.

You may be asking yourself, what can I do before I get married? First, you need to analyze where your money is going. You also need to talk to your spouse-to-be about his or her finances. Do your background research to get credit reports, FICO scores, and a history of bill payments (for you and spouse). You should both get your information and share it with each other. Remember, once you are married, you are assuming responsibility for your spouse's debt as well. If your spouse or spouse-to-be is better at the finances than you, maybe they should be in charge of them; however, the main point to remember is that we all have to take responsibility for our actions and ensure the household finances are taken care of.

One suggestion for people who are preparing for marriage is to get professional premarital counseling. A good counselor will help you prepare for marriage. An additional form of counseling I would recommend is sitting down with a financial advisor/planner. There are many places where you can get a free consultation. I would definitely recommend a free consultation, but if none are available, paying a small fee for a good, sound financial plan is not a bad deal. A good plan will allow you to discuss long-term goals and how to achieve them. Good insurance programs should be discussed along with short-term goals and requirements. If you are not used to preparing for the future, this meeting will open your eyes.

The intent of this chapter is to make sure you plan for marriage in more ways than just on the emotional level. Finances play a major part in our lives, and even though the love of money causes problems, the lack of money causes problems as well. Marriage is a continual effort by two people to become one, and the fewer problems there are, the easier and happier your marriage will be.

19

I'M MARRIED...
NOW WHAT?

This chapter continues from the previous one. If you are already married, it is not too late to get your finances in order. If you were able to follow the guidelines set out in the previous chapter, your marriage will be smoother in the beginning; however, if you didn't, it is not too late to get off on the right foot. By following the guidelines from previous chapters, you already know to pay charity, pay yourself, and pay your bills.

As a married couple, you must establish a strict budget and follow it to improve your financial situation. You should make sure your needs are taken care of first. Once you've donated to charitable organizations, paid yourself (investments), and paid your bills, you can now allocate money for some of your wants. Notice that I said "some of your wants." I'll say it again—*some* of your wants. And then only after all of your other responsibilities have been taken care of. This means you have to pay cash for your wants. Credit cards are not for your wants. Really, credit cards are not for needs either. If you have your budget properly set up, you can have money for your needs, some wants, and for any emergency that may come your way.

Every business operates from a budget on an annual basis. If it works for them, it'll work for us as well. My wife and I follow a budget. We have to constantly adjust where our money goes, but at least we have a plan on paper for where we wish to allocate our money. It works very well, and it also serves as a historical account of where your money was actually spent. We have everything from the house payment, investments, gasoline, and personal allowance listed in our budget. Yes, we actually budget our allowance, but I haven't seen one in a while due to other obligations. My wife on the other hand, has a higher priority than me. Trust me, women are going to get their hair done. I have a few sets of hair clippers that I use for cutting my hair. As I think about it, it's funny. We live a comfortable lifestyle, and if I want something, my wife will make sure I have it. On paper, my allowance says I can't have it, but you can always find a few dollars somewhere. If you use a budget, you'll curb some spending habits while increasing the amount of money available for investments, savings, and extra payments on current debt.

This is a financial book, but it is full of other information that will assist you on your path to success. One area that can be overlooked is the company you keep. (Yeah, I'm going there . . .) If you want to get anywhere in life, you cannot allow negative people to keep you from progressing. I'm not saying to totally "blow off" anyone who doesn't think like you, but you don't need to have friends who are not trying to go the same direction you are. The reason I say this is because people tend to become the people they are around. If you are around highly motivated, successful people, you will eventually possess some of their qualities. If you are constantly around people who always are going through issues, their problems can somehow rub off on you as well. You can still associate with them and hopefully you will be able to instill some of your values into them. The main point is: 1) You have to watch the people you are friends with; 2) whether discussing marriage or finances, you don't want to have other people's problems affecting you and your spouse; and 3) your spouse is your best friend now (not your other male or female friends). I hope you can read into the words that were just stated. Keep your family safe by stopping problems from coming into your home!

Can I speak to the men again for a second? The bottom line is that we are men. God made us the head of the family, and we are to love our wives like Christ loved the church. Christ gave his life for us despite all the bad things we ever did, and despite the fact that we still stumble at times. We must love our wives the same way. We must sacrifice for our wives as well. By doing this, you, your wife, and your entire family will be blessed. When your wife is happy, you will be happy. If your wife sees that you are unselfish and always provide for her before you satisfy your own desires, she will make sure you have some of the things you want as well. It can be an adjustment going from being able to buy whatever you want, whenever you want it, to placing someone else's needs and desires ahead of your own. This is a shock for men and women, but women tend to have the motherly touch automatically instilled in them.

The Bible says in Proverbs 13:22: "A good man leaveth an inheritance to his children's children: and the wealth of the sinner is laid up for the just." That is a powerful scripture. We are to pass on wealth to our grandchildren. Many people only pass on debt and have others scrambling to pay for the funeral. It doesn't have to be this way. Readjust your financial baseline and store wealth to pass on to future generations.

Men, we have to lead by example. Your family doesn't have to have everything to be happy. My wife and I sacrifice every day. We sacrificed when we first were married and continue to do so. In the beginning of our marriage, we sacrificed because we had no choice. A lot of our money went to car payments and insurance. Later, we began sacrificing to fund our Individual Retirement Accounts

(IRAs) and 401(k)s. At one point, we proved that we could live on one income comfortably. We also started multiple businesses during and after my military career. Our businesses are investments for our long-term financial future. A business will also open your eyes to other options you can pursue in the future. Keep your mind open to explore all business options, and when your spouse has a good idea, don't shut them down.

One piece of advice I will give couples is to give and take. Be prepared to give up some things you like and to have your spouse take some things you may not have had to share in the past. I'm not saying you have to share your toothbrush, but you should be willing to sacrifice whatever is necessary to make sure your marriage works. Marriage is what you make of it, and you get out of it what you put into it. Marriage is fun, and it is even more fun when you have money in the bank. Trust me on that one!

20

IT'S UP
TO YOU!

A strong financial future begins with a solid foundation. The budget is the most overlooked part of that foundation. Companies and governments have budgets, but for many people, money is spent without accounting for it. I am a firm believer of not spending more than you take in. This includes money you spend and save for the long term.

There are many financial tools, including books, websites, and seminars, that can aid you on your path to financial freedom. This book should only be the beginning of your quest to get you where you want to be in a certain amount of time. Make sure you set realistic goals, and reward yourself (not to the point of indulgence) for accomplishing your goals. Spread the word to others about how they can become financially independent as well. Once you are able to pay all of your bills, invest for the future, and help others and yourself the way you truly want to, you will be glad you took these simple steps. One of my supervisors always told me, "Small rudder inputs move the ship to land." To put it in financial terms, small sacrifices and discipline over a period of time will put you where you really want and need to be.

Some people do not want to do what it takes to have a prosperous future. It is easy to say what you need to do, but many lack the motivation and discipline to put words into action. Whether dealing with personal, business, or organizational finances, financial discipline is a must in order to get ahead. Ten years from now, you should be in a better financial state than you are in now. You should be progressing toward your goals. You may have minor set-backs, but if you properly prepare for the future you can take the minor issues head on.

Everyone has different goals and desires. Remember, it's up to you!

21

SUPPORT A CAUSE
YOU BELIEVE IN

Life is not just about you! While there is nothing wrong with enjoying life, you should also make it a point to help others. For example, as I mentioned, my mother died of breast cancer when I was six years old. I have made it a point to help others facing cancer. At times, we donate to the large organizations, and we have also directly donated to individuals undergoing cancer treatment and even paid their insurance premiums. This is near to my heart since my mother lost her battle. Whatever I can do to help others during their difficult time, I feel like it is a small sacrifice for me.

When you give, you will receive. When you open your hand to give, you enable something to be placed in your hand. While we should not give expecting to receive, it is critical that giving of ourselves become a part of who we are. Many successful individuals find ways to have a big impact on others' lives. Find a way to support others that gives meaning and fulfills a need.

While financial support will always be welcome, organizations also can benefit from your time and experience. You can be a mentor or just encourage someone who needs it. There are opportunities to assist with schools, churches, and other organizations. The main point is that you are not to keep your knowledge to yourself; make it a point to share your knowledge with others. Make it a point to provide knowledge to others.

As I said before, I strongly desired to fly for the Air Force. Despite being selected to become an Air Force pilot, the Air Force decided not to let me fly due to vision deficiencies. At the time, my deficiency was not allowed but later on, people with my condition were allowed to fly. Even though I was not able to fly for the Air Force, I knew what it took to get selected. I mentored two individuals, and they both became military pilots. One joined the Navy, and the other flew for the Air Force. The point is that even if you don't reach your goal in a certain area, you can still assist others to fulfill their dreams.

22

YOUR STRATEGY FOR SUCCEEDING AT LIFE

People's definition of success can differ, and that's fine. Whether you desire to become an attorney, pilot, educator, or business owner, you must take the proper steps to pave the way for you to reach success, however you define it. While parents often teach children to work hard, there are also some other things you should know that can help you.

Education is important, but do not fall victim to amassing so much student loan debt you will never be able to pay it back. It is okay to attend a community college and transfer to a four-year university to save money. Personally, I utilized military training, community college courses, and "testing out" to obtain credit for classes without taking them. According to my records, I passed eight classes (twenty-four college hours) utilizing testing to obtain college credit. I saved time and money!

We also need to change our thought processes. You can be successful despite your background or whether or not your family was well off. You have the power to change things. Make sure you use it! Do not worry about others who may seem to be enjoying life. Do not compare yourself to others! Set you own goals and take the necessary steps to accomplish them. You may want to become a business owner instead of working for a corporation. You may choose to become a teacher instead of a more high-paying position with a large company. It doesn't matter which path you choose. Make sure you enjoy what you do and become the best at it.

Find out what really drives you. Do you choose money or happiness? Remember, not everyone is wired the same way. Some may want money while others may want happiness. The main thing is to prepare in order to reach whatever aspiration you have. For example, if you desire to become a millionaire, you will have to save early and consistently to reach your goal. Someone who just wants to be out of debt may be less ambitious about saving, but they are both working toward a good goal. Find your goal, and make sure you work toward it.

While working toward your goal, it is important to always give back and support a cause you believe in. For example, I support various organizations that help people who are facing multiple illnesses. This is something I do because of my mom losing her battle to cancer. It allows me to take a little stress off someone and give them hope while they or their loved ones are fighting to be healed.

Succeeding at life is really up to you. Determine what your definition of success is and work toward it. You are more than able to complete this task. I believe in you.

FINDING YOUR ROAD | PATH | SUCCESS IN LIFE

Below are four keys to succeeding at life. It is essential that you take care of yourself in order to reach your full potential. I provided the points below when I spoke to high school graduates, and they are definitely still relevant for you as well.

1. Find Your Dream | Mission | Purpose | Passion
2. Launch Out into the Deep | The Unknown—Best Opportunity to Learn
3. Nurture Your Passion
4. Do Not Quit

Additional Page for Your Notes

HOME BUYING &
WEALTH BUILDING

23

FATHER, WHERE IS
MY INHERITANCE?

The Bible states in Proverbs 13:22 that "a good man leaveth an inheritance to his children's children . . ." An inheritance is often referred to as a large sum of money "gifted" to a loved one, but there are four types of inheritances fathers are responsible for. Spiritual, physical, emotional, and financial inheritances are critical to equip our children to become successful leaders in our society. If we do not provide inheritances, our children could face emotional and economic struggles in the future. First Timothy 5:8 states, "But if any provide not for his own, and specifically for those of his own house, he hath denied the faith, and is worse than an infidel." According to the *Webster's II New College Dictionary*, "infidel" is defined as "one without religious beliefs."

The most important inheritance, the spiritual inheritance, involves demonstrating the love of God for our children and building their foundation. Today, many children are not developing a true relationship with God because their fathers are lacking a committed relationship with God as well. Fathers, we owe it to ourselves and our children to provide them a solid spiritual inheritance.

The physical inheritance ensures our children are protected and allowed to grow and mature into adults. Fathers, we are responsible for providing a safe, secure, and loving environment. God has trusted us with precious children, and we must protect them from all dangers using both physical and intellectual means. Being a protective father will lessen the chance that molestation or tragic accidents will occur. Without providing a good physical inheritance, the financial inheritance will be worthless, and you may end up providing more economic assistance to your child over their lifetime.

The emotional inheritance is one where we often fall short. With all of the ongoing issues in the world, our children must know their fathers love them. They should know their fathers truly have their backs (even when we have to enforce discipline). By providing love, our children will be able to face obstacles in school, college, the workforce, and wherever they find themselves. The importance of emotional support in our children's lives should not be minimized. Fathers, step up and provide the emotional support our children are so often lacking. If we do not step up, they'll attempt to get it from sources that are not beneficial to them.

The financial inheritance involves providing economic resources to our children. Fathers, we must put something aside consistently for our children to ensure they can obtain the best education and are provided a head start in life. Stocks and real estate are common forms of investing, but another way to provide a financial inheritance is to start and own a business. There are many options available, and the sooner we begin saving for our children's future, the larger the inheritance will grow.

We must provide our children with spiritual, physical, emotional, and financial inheritances to fulfill our purpose and be considered great fathers. By placing our children ahead of us, we will make the best decisions and provide the inheritances they rightly deserve. It is not too late to correct the past. If you have not been an active father providing an inheritance for your children, you can start today! This is critical in order to build and pass on wealth to future generations.

24

BUILDING
WEALTH . . . ONE
HOME AT A TIME

Many times, people read without taking action; however, this chapter is different. Instead of just being interesting reading material, this chapter will tell you how you can get involved to build wealth . . . one home at a time.

Building wealth should be a part of everyone's financial plan, and one way to build wealth is through home ownership. Yes, there are additional costs involved with maintaining a home, but being able to enjoy an asset that historically appreciates in value is a wise decision. When you decide to purchase a home, utilizing a fifteen-year mortgage will allow you to own your property in half the time of a traditional thirty-year mortgage. This may require you to purchase a less expensive home than you would have qualified for with a thirty-year mortgage, but it will put you on the fast track to building wealth.

Austin Luxury Realty Services sponsors Home & Wealth Building Cohorts consisting of people who plan to buy homes at

some point in the future as well as those who have already purchased homes. The intent is to provide a roadmap for homebuyers
and also offer additional guidance once people have purchased
homes. Financial consulting, credit repair, credit score reviewing,
budgeting, and other topics are taught and discussed to ensure
that people stay on track for their homeownership plans. For those
who have already purchased a home, strategies are provided that, if
implemented, will assist clients with paying their homes off early,
eliminating debt, and increasing their net worth.

Austin Luxury Realty Services has partnered with organizations
across the country to plan for the large number of clients utilizing the cohort program. Our goal is to have a powerful, positive
impact on our communities by allowing families to increase the
health of their personal finances and build wealth. While the focus
is to increase the net worth of our communities, we still encourage
people to enjoy life.

Everyone should have a plan to increase their net worth each
year. While increasing your net worth may not be a quick process,
it is well worth the time involved. Being committed and changing
your ways will allow you and your family to prosper for years to
come. Remember, during these drastic economic times, we must
take drastic measures to achieve financial success. Your future
depends on it!

25

HOME
BUYING
STEPS

Basics of a Mortgage:

- ➜ Know Your Target (Estimated) Purchase Price (2.5 to 3 Times Your Annual Income)
- ➜ Apply for a Loan with a Lender
- ➜ Know Your Estimated Credit Score—Lender Will Pull Your Score Prior to Issuing a Pre-Qualification or Pre-Approval

Qualify for a Loan without a 20-Percent Down Payment:

There are a variety of public and private lenders who, if you qualify, offer mortgages that require a small down payment.

Conventional: 5% | FHA: 3.5% | VA: 0% | USDA: 0%

Earnest Money: Typically, between 1 to 3 percent of purchase price; some builders can be as low as $500 (need to be prepared to provide the money when the contract is written)

Save Money for Down Payment | Closing Costs

Down payment figures are above and depend on the type of loan you are utilizing. Closing costs are separate from the down payment requirement, and can be negotiated. It is wise to attempt to have the seller pay your closing costs. Many variables determine your closing cost figures, and your lender will provide the exact figures to you. Closing costs can range from approximately 3 percent to 5 percent. Again, these figures depend on the cost of the fees involved, taxes, etc.

Proper Planning:

→ No new purchases
→ Reduce debt
→ Save money

Obtain Loan Pre-Approval or Pre-Qualification:

We highly recommend you obtain a pre-approval or pre-qualification prior to your home search. Once you know the amount the lender approves or qualifies you for, you can then set realistic expectations for your new home.

Some lenders will issue a pre-approval early in the process. This is a more strict process than a pre-qualification and takes your file through the underwriting process. All that will remain for you to do is to find your home, write a contract, and have the contract added to your file.

A pre-qualification is normally used and is based on a cursory review of your finances, income, debt, and credit history. Once you have a contract for your home, the lender will begin the actual loan approval process.

Decide What Qualities You Desire in a Home:

Answer the following questions to narrow home search:
→ Estimated Purchase Price:
→ Square Footage Desired:

ESTIMATED BUYER'S COST WORKSHEET

Property Address _____

_____

_____

Sales Price: _____

Down Payment: _____

Amount Financed: _____

Buyer's Costs: _____

LOAN ITEMS:

Loan Originating Fee: $ _____
Appraisal Fee: $ _____
Credit Report: $ _____
Additional Loan Fees: $ _____

PREPAID ITEMS:

Interest: $ _____
Hazard Insurance: $ _____
Mortgage Insurance: $ _____
Taxes: $ _____
Assessments: $ _____
Other Fees: $ _____

TITLE AND CLOSING CHARGES:

Escrow, Settlement, Closing Fee: $ _____
Title Insurance: $ _____

Notary Fee: $ _____
Attorney's Fee: $ _____
Other Fees: $ _____

RECORDING FEES:

Recording Fees: $ _____
Tax Stamps: $ _____
Other Fees: $ _____

ADDITIONAL SETTLEMENT CHARGES:

Survey: $_____
Pest Inspection: $_____
Home Warranty: $_____
Home Inspection Fee: $_____

TOTAL SETTLEMENT CHARGES:

Down Payment: $_____
Total Estimate Buyers Cost: $_____
Amount Financed: $_____
Interest Rate: _____%
Term: _____ years

ESTIMATED MONTHLY PAYMENT:

Principal & Interest: $_____
Mortgage Insurance (PMI)
(if any): $_____
Property Taxes: $_____
Homeowner's Insurance: $_____
Homeowner's Assoc. Fee
(if any): $_____

TOTAL MONTHLY PAYMENT:

_____

Note: This is an estimate only. Accurate payment information should be attained from your lender. Payments are not guaranteed by Austin Luxury Realty Services or your Sales Agent.

- ➤ Single Story or Two Story:
- ➤ Number of Bedrooms:
- ➤ Number of Bathrooms:
- ➤ Additional Rooms Desired (media, game room, study, etc):
- ➤ Interior Layout (open layout, etc):
- ➤ Age of Home (pre-owned, new construction, etc):
- ➤ Any Additional Specific Details You Desire in a Home:
- ➤ Decide on the Location/Area(s) You Desire to Search for a Home in:

Begin Your Home Search:
- ➤ View recurring emails with homes that fit criteria
- ➤ Select your favorite/potential homes
- ➤ Schedule dates/times to view properties

Do Your Homework before Making an Offer:
- ➤ Offer should be based on sales trend of similar homes in the area
- ➤ View comparative market analysis that considers sales of similar homes in the last six months

Write Contract | Offer on Home:
- ➤ Turn contract in to mortgage loan officer
- ➤ Home inspection determines repairs needed prior to closing
- ➤ Lender appraisal calculates home's value; at least purchase price

Closing:
Typically closing is 30–45 days after contract is written (unless building a new home)

Advantages of Using Real Estate Broker | Agent:
- ➤ You have representation throughout the process
- ➤ As a buyer, there is no charge to you
- ➤ The seller typically pays the entire commission

26

MORTGAGE
PROCESS

Pre-Approval | Purchasing Power:

Mortgage Professional reviews:
- ➤ Credit Worthiness
- ➤ Employment History / Income
- ➤ Assets

Home Shopping:

Go Over Estimated Payments / Closing Costs:
- ➤ Breakdown of Monthly Payment
- ➤ What Can Be Expected at Closing

Documents Needed (sample only—lenders have their exact requirements):

Identity Verification:
- ➤ Copy of IDs

Income Verification:
- One-month paystubs (most recent)
- Two months bank statements, all pages of all accounts
- Last two years of W-2s, K-1s, and/or 1099s as applicable
- Last two years of tax returns, all pages and all schedules; if self-employed two years business returns will be needed as well

Asset Verification:
- Mortgage statement on any real estate owned or proof that it is free and clear (if applicable)
- Proof of taxes and insurance on any real estate owned (if applicable)
- Divorce Decree, all pages, signed by judge (if applicable)

Loan Submitted:

After your home purchase contract is accepted:
- Mortgage Professional Reviews Contract
- Discuss Interest Rates and Remaining Process
- Loan Submitted to Processing and Underwriting

Underwriting:

Underwriter Reviews:
- Credit History | Contract | Loan Program | Income and Employment History
- Qualified Assets | Appraisal | Regulatory Compliance

Processing:

Lender Team Will:
- Review Conditional Approval list—Gather Items
- Order Title
- Make Sure Appraisal Stays on Task If Not Back from Appraisal

- Management Company
- Coordinate with IRS for Tax Transcripts
- Work on Home Owner's Insurance Policy
- Work with Underwriter on Any Exceptions Needed

Closing Team / Department:

Closing Team Handles:
- Final Disclosures
- Coordinate with Legal to Ensure Loan Is Compliant
- Coordinate with Title Company, Agents, Buyers and Sellers
- Arranges Closing Time and Date Once **"Clear to Close"** Is Received

Final Document Signing:

Sign Final Documents at Title Company | **Receive Your Keys!**

27

UNDERSTANDING CREDIT & IMPROVING CREDIT SCORES

What Is Credit:

- ➤ Using someone else's money to pay for things
- ➤ A promise to repay the money (the debt)
- ➤ Usually involves paying with interest

Two (2) Types of Credit

- ➤ Secured
- ➤ Unsecured

Secured vs. Unsecured Debt:

Secured Debt:

- ➤ Purchases made where the debt is "tied" to the item you purchased
- ➤ Car | Jewelry | Appliances | Home
- ➤ If you don't pay, lender has right to take property back

Unsecured Debt:

- ➤ Purchases made where the debt is "not tied" to any purchase item you make
- ➤ Vacation using credit card | Dinner on credit | Clothing on credit
- ➤ Lender can't take vacation back but credit score will suffer

Efficient Use of Credit:

- ➤ Keep debt-to-income ratio low (~40% or lower)
- ➤ Debt-to-income ratio: monthly debt divided by monthly income
- ➤ Example: $2,000 debt / $4,000 income = 50% debt-to-income ratio
- ➤ Pay your bills on time
- ➤ Only apply for the credit you need
- ➤ Make a list of all debts: Issuer | Balances | Interest rates | Due dates
- ➤ Tackle each debt one at a time
- ➤ Pay off debt with highest interest rate or with lowest balance

Credit Card Utilization:

- ➤ Do not apply for new credit before applying for home loan
- ➤ Check credit card statement against receipts every month
- ➤ Keep the balance less than 25% of the maximum limit
- ➤ Pay off card every month | Building credit—leave a small balance to show usage
- ➤ Always pay more than the minimum payment
- ➤ Mail payments at least 5 business days before due date or use online payments
- ➤ If you move, notify creditors at least 30 days in advance

What Are Credit Scores?:

- ➤ Computer model prediction on how likely an individual will repay a debt
- ➤ Scores based on experience with millions of consumers

→ Computer model assigns points to information on a **credit report**

QUESTION: Do you know your credit score?

How Do Credit Scores Affect Me?:
- → Lower credit scores = higher interest rates on credit/loans
- → Scores below 600 can prevent you from buying a home

What Determines Credit Score:
- → Payment history—35% | Amounts owed—30%
- → Length of credit history—15% | New credit—10% | Types of credit used—10%

How to Improve Your Credit Score:
- → Check your reports on a regular basis
- → Pay bills on time
  - + If not current, get current and stay current
- → Keep debt low
  - + Don't simply move debt around—pay it off
  - + Don't close unused credit card accounts
  - + Don't open a number of new accounts to increase available credit
- → Check your limits
- → Dispute errors on credit report
  - + Fixing a credit score only pertains to errors
  - + Be careful removing negative items older than 7 years due to the potential impact on your credit score | Speak with a professional

Credit Tips:
- → Negotiate lower interest rate or payment plan with creditors
- → Avoid debt consolidation companies
- → Keep balances below 25% of available credit limit

- Be careful about cosigning
- Do not let banks increase your credit limits
- Live within your means
- Seek reputable help | Credit repair companies can help

What Is in Your Credit Report?:

Identifying information
- Your name | Current & previous address
- Birth date | Social Security number | Current and previous employers
- Public records
- Bankruptcies | Foreclosures | Tax liens | Monetary court judgments
- Collection accounts

Credit accounts (car, mortgage, lines of credit, credit cards, student loans)
- Date opened and closed | Payment history | Balances | Credit limits or loan amounts
- Payment terms | Account status: open vs. closed
- Account type: individual, joint, authorized user
- Age of account

Hard Inquiry (these affect your credit score)
- Applications for a new credit card | Requests to activate a pre-approved credit card
- Activations of new cell phone contracts | Opening new checking or savings account
- Multiple inquiries by home lenders within a short time will count as one inquiry

Soft Inquiry (does not affect your score)
- Credit report and score you request yourself
- Initial credit checks by credit card companies that solicit you

- Initial credit checks by mortgage companies for pre-approval
- Credit background checks by a potential employer
- Periodic credit checks by insurance / credit card company

Disputing an Item on a Report:

- Contact the creditor or credit bureau
- Write a letter of dispute
- Creditor/credit bureau must respond to you within 30 days
- If disagree with finding, can submit a 100-word explanation

FINANCIAL
STEWARDSHIP

Financial stewardship takes place across a wide spectrum. The focus of this chapter is to ensure you are not sacrificing free money and also that you are protecting your investments.

401(k) / 403(b):

- → 401(k): Most common form of investment offered to employees
- → 403(b): Generally offered to employees of public/nonprofit organizations
- → Contribute at least the minimum amount to receive company-sponsored match

Company Match=Free Money!

- → Diversify your investments
- → Company plans often have lower fees than outside investment companies

➤ Can leave money in company plan even if you depart from the company

IRAs:

➤ Traditional IRA:
  ✦ Contributions are tax deductible | Penalty if withdrawn prior to age 59 ½
  ✦ Distributions are taxed when withdrawn
➤ Roth IRA:
  ✦ Contributions are not tax deductible | Distributions are tax-free
  ✦ Can withdraw $10K towards first home purchase | Penalty if withdrawn before 59 ½
  ✦ Can withdraw your principal contributions at any time tax-free and penalty-free

Legal Documents:

➤ Discuss your estate planning with a legal professional
➤ Wills | Trusts
➤ Protect the wealth you work so hard for

Insurance:

➤ Life insurance ensures family taken care of in event of a tragedy

29

INVESTING

Investing is a broad topic. You can invest in everything from savings and money market accounts to stocks and bonds. You can also invest in mutual funds and contribute to employer-sponsored 401(k) accounts. A popular retirement account today is the Roth IRA. This account allows you to pay taxes on the money before you invest it in order for you to make tax-free withdrawals during retirement. For most people who meet the guidelines, this is a good way to invest. It has many other perks such as penalty-free withdrawals to purchase a first home. Consult a good financial advisor to decide which investment is right for you in your particular situation.

One form of investing that people are actively pursuing is real estate properties. We have researched this area and met with active real estate investors to provide more detailed information. One person I know has jumped head first into real estate investing. He managed to use creative financing to purchase single family homes and an apartment complex. He has had some problems with the apartment complex due to its older age, but the single-family homes have been "guaranteed money-makers."

Before a person begins investing in real estate, I recommend they have an emergency fund for their family established consisting of at least six months' salary or at a minimum six months of monthly debt payments. You will also normally have to put 20 percent of the contract price of the property down in order to qualify for financing. Local real estate investment clubs, investors, and building contractors may be able to point you in the right direction for additional financing options.

For single people, you only need to decide what avenue you want to pursue, but for married people, you need to discuss what you are interested in. Whether you are interested in real estate, stocks, mutual funds, or bonds, you need to make sure your spouse agrees with the method you are contemplating. If they are not comfortable with what you have chosen, don't force it on them. It is easier to get something accomplished if both of you are on the same page. If your spouse would prefer to spend money, make gradual adjustments to the budget and place the money in safe investments until the spouse decides they are as willing to sacrifice to invest as you are. One thing I don't want is for marriages to suffer due to this. You and your spouse should read this book together and make the best decisions for you and your family.

One investment I believe is important is to invest in yourself and a good way to do this is to own your own business. This is not something to be taken lightly. It requires a great deal of financial and emotional sacrifice in order to be successful. There are ways to procure an existing business or purchase a franchise in order to increase your chances of remaining in business.

Now that you are ready to begin laying the foundation for your financial future, I want to first of all congratulate you on your decision. One person at a time, one family at a time, is all it takes to build strong people and families in our communities. Strong communities build strong cities and strong cities build strong nations.

When a person decides to build a house, they have to purchase a lot to build the house on. The lot may have to be leveled and prepped in order to lay the concrete foundation. This is how you must look at your finances. You need to purchase the lot you want to build your house on. The "lot" is your goal or goals you wish to achieve in the long term. If your goal is to become a millionaire, you will have to build on a larger lot than someone who is trying to save $100,000. Right now, pick your "lot."

After you have picked your lot—identified your goals—call the cement company to pour the cement, which is like developing a sound budget to reach those goals. Creating that budget may include calling a financial advisor, taking financial classes, or attending seminars run by qualified individuals. Don't pick just any cement company. It should be a reputable company. This means to take your time and adequately develop your budget.

I have referenced building a strong foundation throughout the book. I firmly believe the foundation is the most important part of your financial future. A house can be the largest and most beautiful one on the block, but if the foundation is not stable, the house will collapse. The foundation is not just your cement. In chapter 3, the foundation was identified as the ground beneath your cement. This is true for your finances as well. If you don't have an emergency fund, IRAs, 401(k)s, bonds, stocks, real estate, and other financial investments that provide support to your cement, your financial future is in jeopardy just like a house built on unstable ground.

Another area that is important in building a strong foundation is life insurance. My preference is term life insurance through a respected company. As your financial foundation increases and your children get older, you may not need as much insurance as you did when your children were younger and you had more debt than assets. This is something that can be discussed with a good financial planner.

Now that you have the lot selected and have the investments and insurance needed to lay your cement foundation on your lot, you are on your way to having a strong base on which to build.

One important fact is to make sure your cement is properly leveled to ensure your house is not sloping when it is built. Leveling the cement takes place by ensuring you are investing in the places you need to in the right amounts. A person in their twenties may not need to invest in "safer areas" compared to a person in their fifties. The main difference in your financial foundation compared to a physical building is that you can constantly adjust your financial foundation according to your circumstances; however, don't compromise your financial foundation. It is an important area that needs to be kept strong in any way needed. Your financial foundation, once established, should only need minor changes. Remember, the foundation is the most important part of every structure. Make sure you spend the appropriate amount of time and energy necessary to properly build your foundation. I guarantee you will be appreciative later in life if you prepare for the future right now.

30

SUBTLE MONEY

One evening, a wise young man made a comment that I have continued to think about. He began discussing the term subtle money. He explained that subtle money is not flashy, but if you look closely, you can see it. The fact that a young man even *thought* about subtle money is very remarkable. He is on his way to being a very successful person and no doubt will be a positive influence to all those around him.

The definition of subtle is: "so delicate or precise as to be difficult to analyze or describe; delicately complex and understated." Subtle basically means that something is not obvious. Conservative (a true conservative and not the political term) is another word to describe the act of being subtle.

Subtle money is not flashy or displayed to everyone. It may be in investments, real estate, and, for some, in a coffee can, mattress, or a safe. Subtle money people are the ones who have reached a certain maturity level financially. They realize the importance of wealth versus debt, and they understand that having subtle money is like fertilizer on a yard. The fertilizer is not something to brag about, but when you see how green your yard turns after you apply it, you realize and appreciate its impact. Similar to fertilizer's effect on our yard, subtle money has a lasting impact on our entire financial well-being.

There are people among us who may not look like they have wealth but who actually have secured their financial future. We all should take a more subtle approach with our finances. It is perfectly fine to have luxurious thing we can afford. On the other hand, it is also perfectly fine to be the owner of conservative things and take a more subtle money approach with your finances.

Our society is not based on people living with subtle money. Many people desire to show their wealth (or lack of it) in material things. When you are content with who you are, you will be a better person and will not worry about what you have or do not have. When we as a people and as a country stop measuring our success by how much "stuff" we have, it will make all of us better. Remember, just because you cannot see a person's money, does not mean it is not there. They may have subtle money!

31

YOUR HOME BUYING & WEALTH BUILDING STRATEGY

Real estate historically has been a way to increase an individual's wealth. When incorporated into the overall strategy, it can be a good way to build your solid financial foundation. The primary method for real estate should be purchasing either a single-family home or a multi-family property where you can live in, or at least in one of the units if it's a multi-family property. Since you must have a place to live, you might as well buy a home. While there are additional costs involved with ownership, home appreciation over time will outweigh the costs.

Your home buying strategy should be well thought out. A sound strategy may not allow you to get rich overnight, but if you stay with it, you will reap the benefits. You should desire to buy at a negotiated price and allow the property to increase in value. As your position grows, you can purchase additional properties and employ other investment strategies. For example, you can grow from single-family properties, to buying vacant lots, and later building homes to sell. You may also want to pursue commercial properties as a long-term investment. The most important thing to remember is to not go faster than you can afford to. While it may be tempting to try to make more money by investing in a more expensive or higher risk property, it is crucial to only buy what works for your financial strategy. Just because the lender qualifies you for a certain amount does not mean you should spend that amount.

As far as wealth building goes, your process should be similar to an airplane. In the beginning, it takes a lot of effort to get going. Once you take off, the pilots are actively ensuring the airplane systems are properly performing. Later, when the airplane is at cruising altitude, the pilots level the airplane off and focus on maintaining a steady altitude. At this point, maintaining the altitude does not take as much effort as when the aircraft was taking off. These same principles can be applied to finances. In the beginning, it will take a lot of hard work and may even be painful. Once you get the process going and develop a new normal, things will get better.

Below are four areas that can assist with your home-buying and wealth-building process.

1. Contribute to an Individual Retirement Account and/or Company-Sponsored Investment Fund
2. Purchase an Owner-Occupied Single-Family Property
3. Progress to Purchasing an Investment Property
4. Research and Start a Business

Page for personal notes . . .

Page for personal notes . . .

_____

_____

_____

_____

_____

_____

_____

_____

_____

_____

_____

_____

_____

_____

CONCLUSION

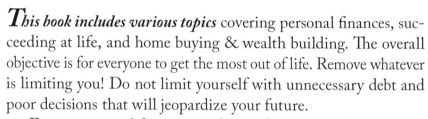

32

STRATEGIES
FOR SUCCESS

This book includes various topics covering personal finances, succeeding at life, and home buying & wealth building. The overall objective is for everyone to get the most out of life. Remove whatever is limiting you! Do not limit yourself with unnecessary debt and poor decisions that will jeopardize your future.

From a personal finance standpoint, I recommend:

- → Developing and utilizing a budget
- → Building and maintaining an emergency fund
- → Preparing for and investing in additional financial investment opportunities
- → Motivating others to reach their full potential

Budgeting is essential. It can help keep you moving in the correct direction. While budgeting is often downplayed, if properly used, it can keep you focused and disciplined, and allow you to account for your money. Corporations use budgets to manage their money and control their spending. Our personal finances should be managed in a similar fashion.

An emergency fund can minimize stress when an unexpected expense arises while also protecting your personal finances. Some people cannot get ahead financially because they are living paycheck to paycheck. Car trouble or any unplanned expense can cripple them financially. Your emergency fund is a must while on your path to financial freedom!

Implementing a good financial strategy is critical to reaching your overall personal financial goals. You can save as much or as little as you desire; however, our recommendation is to be consistent. The more you can save and the longer you can save prior to retirement determine how big your nest egg will be. While you are young, you need to save! This will allow your money a longer timeframe to work for you. If you made mistakes and are trying to get back on track, it is not too late. Begin saving immediately. Reaching the same level in a shorter amount of time may require saving larger amounts, but you can still reach your goals in this way.

You should motivate others to reach their full financial potential. We should not learn something and keep it to ourselves. Good or bad, we should share lessons learned with those around us to prevent them from making the same mistakes we did and also to encourage them to do what also worked for us.

You must take care of yourself to reach your full potential. Four keys to succeeding at life are:

- ➜ Find your purpose
- ➜ Launch out into the deep
- ➜ Nurture your passion
- ➜ Do not quit

You must not wander aimlessly in life—find your purpose! Your purpose, vision, and passion will guide you and give you the desire to want to do your best. Personally, I love helping people. I teach personal finances and home buying, and I have even mentored people in the aviation field. By knowing my purpose, I am able to be more confident and pass my knowledge on to others.

The world is too large to sit in one place your whole life. **Whether it comes naturally or you have to work at it, you must launch out into the deep**. This so-called deep is the unknown. For me, it began by joining the Air Force. I lived in various cities and states while meeting many new people. I gained personal and professional knowledge that has made me who I am today.

You must nurture your passion or it will wither. Just like we must nourish our bodies, we have to constantly nurture our passion to keep it alive. There may be setbacks, delays, and frustrations, and it may seem like you are not moving in the direction you desire. But this is when you must find ways to feed your passion. **Continue to press forward and, most importantly, do not quit**!

Real estate plays an important role in wealth building. Whether you desire to buy a home now or in the future, you should begin planning for it while continuing to invest in other areas to ensure you maximize your ability to build wealth.

Below are four areas that can assist with your home buying & wealth building process:

→ Contribute to an individual retirement account or company-sponsored investment fund
→ Purchase a home for you and your family
→ Progress to purchasing an investment property
→ Research and start a business

A key wealth building method is contributing to retirement accounts. **You should at least contribute the minimum required to obtain any company-sponsored plan match, and contributing to an outside individual retirement account or mutual fund is also a wise decision**.

Purchasing a single-family home to reside in can be an excellent starting point for many individuals. As your wealth and earning ability grows, you can **progress to buying investment properties that can include multi-family, commercial, and even land**.

You should desire to continuously grow your wealth, and another potential way to do so is by **owning a business**. I'm not advocating that you buy an expensive business just so you can say you are a business owner; however, if you have a talent or ability that can generate an additional stream of income (even while you are employed), this can be another approach to building wealth.

Thanks for reading this book. Hosea 4:6 states, "My people are destroyed for the lack of knowledge . . ." This book provides knowledge you can implement in your life and also pass to others. If properly utilized, the strategies we've discussed will help put you on the path to financial freedom. I wish you the best with all of your endeavors!

APPENDIX

INFORMATION FOR
ACTIVE DUTY MILITARY
AND VETERANS

This chapter is unique in that the data will be specifically for military members. If you are not in the military, this chapter will still provide key data for you to use and share with others. Everyone knows someone in the military, and even if they don't have the book, you can provide them with good information to act upon. This information will enable them to have a good career and not worry about how their family will survive if something happens to them. It will also address what needs to be done in case of a deployment, as well as educational opportunities available. I have taken advantage of several programs that allowed me to get to where I am today. The final section of this chapter will address military retirement. We'll show what military retirement can provide for you and how it should play a part in your long-term retirement plan. For those who don't plan to make the military a career, we'll address what you should do to plan for a comfortable exit at your convenience.

Insurance is a sore subject for many people. First of all, people are scared to face the fact that something may cut their life short. We hope and pray that each and every one of us lives a long life, but insurance is needed just in case the unspeakable happens.

A military career is a noble one where you are surrounded by very motivated and intelligent individuals. The Bible states in John 15:13, "Greater love hath no man than this, that a man lay down his life for his friends." I do not like the fact that our profession is so dangerous, but we can ensure our families are taken care of if something were to happen.

Educational Benefits

No matter for what reason people decide to enter the military, education is an important part of the picture. There are many different opportunities available to further your education as a member of the military. I'll explain how I utilized various programs to further my education as well as my career.

I signed-up for the Air Force during the fall of my senior year in high school under the delayed entry program. Less than two months after graduating from high school, I went to basic training at Lackland AFB in San Antonio, Texas, on July 12, 1995. I graduated from basic training in August 1995 and was assigned to Keesler AFB in Biloxi, Mississippi, for a ten-month technical school for the aircraft command, control, communication, and navigation course. One note I have to make is that I graduated with a 4.52 GPA out of 5.00; however, I felt like I didn't want to go to school right away, Once I joined the military, my path was chosen for me, and the military decided that I would be in school for a while. After graduating from a ten-month technical training school (with a 90 average), I had orders to Offutt AFB near Omaha, Nebraska.

Shortly after arriving, I began taking college courses. To my surprise, all of the training I had completed for the military transferred as part of my degree program. Visit your education office for specific details on how to transfer your coursework. For me, I was able to transfer approximately fifty-four semester credit hours of military coursework into my degree. I also took CLEP and DANTES tests to obtain college credit simply by taking exams showing I had the necessary knowledge to receive credit for courses I had not taken. I definitely earned my degree in a non-traditional manner and graduated with my bachelor's degree four years after graduating high school with only $8,000 in student loan debt. The military paid my tuition, but I was in a pilot training program that I paid for out of pocket. Yes, I have a private pilot's license with over 100 hours of flight time. I briefly mentioned earlier my struggles with the Air Force about my vision, but for me to fully explain why I didn't fly for the Air Force is a different story and will have to be covered in a different book. My good friend, Horace and I are going to put words to paper about our flying experiences at a later date. We both love flying and want to share the experience with as many people that we can!

I hope my story about how I earned my degree inspires you to reach for the stars. I'm an example of being able to do anything if you put your mind to it. One important note not stated earlier is that for my last two semesters, I went to school full-time for my military job as part of the Bootstrap program. This entitled me to continue receiving my normal military pay. I worked my college schedule to where I attended school Tuesday, Wednesday, and Thursday. I had a four-day weekend every week for one of my semesters. The program has since changed (as far as the benefits are concerned), but it is still an avenue to use for completing your degree quicker. There are other programs to allow you to enter the health, legal, and many other fields as well. Be diligent and conduct research to find the program that will aid you in progressing to where you want to be.

After completing your degree, you can apply for a commission (to become an officer) if you so desire. Another way to become an officer is through ROTC. Again, talk to your education office personnel for more details.

If you decide to exit the military, you can at least take all of your education and use it to help provide for you and your family. DO NOT wait until you get out of the military to go to college. Begin before you depart the military in order to take advantage of the vast educational opportunities at little or no cost to you. The Post 9/11 G.I. Bill is another opportunity you should plan to utilize for educational needs. You can use it for traditional education and also for vocational training. You also receive a housing stipend if attending college more than part-time. You should definitely research and use this well-deserved benefit.

Financial Benefits

Few join the military to become wealthy, but with proper planning, you can enjoy your career while building wealth. The military pay structure is clearly defined, and you and everyone else knows exactly how much each rank earns. In order to receive more pay, you must advance in rank.

I began at the lowest rank in the military, E-1. After obtaining college degrees and completing military training and moves, I ended my career as a Field Grade Officer. While the pay for me was higher on the officer side than on the enlisted side, we need quality people on both sides. Also, for those who advance to the highest enlisted rank and stay for a longer time, they can achieve a nice active duty pay which will translate to a good retirement as well.

Insurance

Many people are uncomfortable about discussing insurance because it is planning for something they hope will never happen. We all hope the insurance will not be needed, but it is important to protect your family and assets in the event something happens to you. The military offers SGLI insurance at a reduced rate to military members. You can also purchase optional spousal coverage at affordable rates. The insurance rates are based on age just like normal policies are, but I encourage you to do your research to ensure you have enough coverage for your family. If you are the only income earner and have young children, you may need at least $750,000 to ensure bills are paid off, money to live off of is allocated, and your children have money for college tuition. The government is not going to take care of your family the way they should be taken care of, so it is our responsibility to ensure their needs and wants are addressed.

Sitting down with a good financial planner can show you where you are and where you should be with your insurance needs. There are many military friendly companies that will allow you to purchase additional insurance coverage, and these policies may pay a certain amount when the first spouse passes away. The fees for most of the policies are affordable, and remember that this is a small sacrifice to provide protection for your family if it is ever needed. If something happens to us, our families are going to grieve because of the pain of losing a loved one. Don't add additional grief because they don't have money to survive! It is up to you to protect your family.

Deployments

Deployments can be long or short. They can be to a nice location or to a desolate area. If you are in the military, chances are you are likely to be deployed. Some may deploy more than others, but the main point is that your family needs to be ready to function with you away.

In many households, one person handles all of the finances. If the finance person is on a deployment, additional stress is placed on the spouse left behind. The deployed person may also worry about whether or not their loved one will pay the bills on time, but it doesn't have to be this way.

I developed a spreadsheet that shows when the bills are due and what check they are paid with, lists the accounts (checking, savings, and investments), displays birthdays, and includes an asset and liability tracker. If I had to leave, my wife could take the sheet and function with no problems. She could probably do it without the sheet, but it provides more peace of mind by having something at her fingertips. I recommend you do the same for your loved one. It can also be used while you are around. We track it and monitor where our money is going and where we actually want it to go. Trust me, looking at where your money goes will make you have second thoughts before you spend it.

Travel Perks

Outside of traditional military deployments to support ongoing military operations, you will also have the opportunity to move to different places to live when you join different units. I highly recommend that you try to enjoy these opportunities. My family and I enjoyed visiting amusement parks, historical landmarks, etc., throughout our time in different areas. You can also take advantage of military travel opportunities using Space-A (Available) transportation using military aircraft to reduce vacation expenses. You'll need to be flexible, but it can be a rewarding experience while saving money.

Real Estate

One successful individual that provided mentoring advice to me told me that whenever you move to a different military assignment, you should attempt to buy real estate every time. While it may not be feasible when moving to a high-cost area, this practice can help you build wealth. By using your military VA Loan benefit, you can buy a home with no money down. Your benefit can be reused if the full benefit has not been utilized, and it can also be fully restored if you sell the property or refinance it to a different type of loan (Conventional, FHA, etc.). The main point is not to wait until you retire or separate from the military to begin your real estate investment. The fact that you can use your tax-free, military housing allowance to pay for your home while you live there should make the decision automatic for you.

Veteran Friendly States

Many states offer extra benefits to military veterans. For example, some states offer disabled veterans some or all property tax exemptions (depending on what percentage disability you have). Some states also offer additional educational benefits for veterans and their dependents. While these benefits vary from state to state, be sure to research your state to see what benefits they offer.

Military Retirement Pay

If you invest, save, and also choose to make the military a career, the military retirement pay can and should be included in your retirement planning. Retirement pay worth hundreds or thousands of dollars a month will reduce the amount of money needed in your investments to produce a desired amount of income for you. If you don't have retirement pay, you may need hundreds of thousands of dollars in an investment fund in order to withdraw the equivalent amount of money during your retirement years. For example, if you wanted to retire with $5,000 a month of income, and your military retirement pay is $3,000 a month, you only need enough money in your investments to cover $2,000 for the rest of your life. The amount needed will vary based on age and life expectancy, but let's assume you'll need about $300,000. Without the retirement pay, your investments would have to cover the entire $5,000. With this scenario, you may need closer to $750,000 in your investments. We all plan differently and need to be aware that although the retirement pay may not be a lot, it will provide supplemental income for the rest of your life. I suggest you research your military resources for retirement information. Various publications targeting the military will publish what your retirement is worth monthly or annually at various times during the year. If you work for twenty years, you can always begin a second career with another employer or for yourself. Personally, I planned and decided to work for myself.

There have been changes to the military retirement system since I retired. They now offer a 401(k)-style system as an option for those who desire to have more flexibility. The military will place certain amounts of money in the fund and offer a reduced military pension. Do your research.

Active Duty & Veteran Strategy:

1. Follow Instructions
2. Develop Your Own Plan | Roadmap
3. Stay Focused | Determined
4. Always Do Your Best